THE Peached TORTILLA

ESTᴰ 10

MODERN ASIAN COMFORT FOOD
FROM TOKYO TO TEXAS

ERIC SILVERSTEIN

STERLING EPICURE
New York

STERLING EPICURE
New York

An Imprint of Sterling Publishing Co., Inc.
1166 Avenue of the Americas
New York, NY 10036

STERLING EPICURE and the distinctive Sterling Epicure logo are registered trademarks of Sterling Publishing Co., Inc.

ISBN 978-1-4549-3121-8

Distributed in Canada by Sterling Publishing Co., Inc.
c/o Canadian Manda Group, 664 Annette Street
Toronto, Ontario M6S 2C8, Canada
Distributed in the United Kingdom by GMC Distribution Services
Castle Place, 166 High Street, Lewes, East Sussex BN7 1XU, England
Distributed in Australia by NewSouth Books
University of New South Wales, Sydney, NSW 2052, Australia

For information about custom editions, special sales, and premium and corporate purchases, please contact Sterling Special Sales at 800-805-5489 or specialsales@sterlingpublishing.com.

Manufactured in Canada

2 4 6 8 10 9 7 5 3

sterlingpublishing.com
thepeachedtortilla.com

Cover design by Elizabeth Lindy
Interior design by Gavin Motnyk

*To Kris, Niko, Jetta, and my family for supporting
my dream over all of these years*

*To my friends, who believed in my venture
and backed me from the beginning*

*To my staff, for grinding day in and day out
to make our business a success*

CONTENTS

FOREWORD

I met Eric Silverstein back in 2010 at the San Francisco Street Food Festival. I'll be honest: I haven't met a lot of Chinese dudes with a Southern drawl, but he had that easygoing and relaxed demeanor that was Texas through and through. Chinese Texas, that is. Here we were, two street food guys, myself from Seattle and Eric from Austin, Texas, doing the hustle and trying to grab the opportunity in front of us in life.

While at this event, where Eric was making something like two thousand portions of tacos in the course of a day, it became very apparent that he was someone who worked his ass off. I still remember him in the commissary mixing big buckets of peanut sauce in this kitchen that was a complete shitshow, and he was utterly focused. To paint the picture a bit more, this was a group of street food vendors in a tiny kitchen, and let's just say, at these types of events, it is like a mix of "carnies," cat-herding, and screaming-hot ovens, but there was Eric over his bucket of peanut sauce . . . locked in . . . focused.

Years later, after I had opened my first brick-and-mortar, there was a moment when Eric and I were talking. He mentioned that he was also thinking of opening a restaurant, down in Austin. I told him to go for it and not to even think twice about it. Street food is hard, and the kind of work that it entails is unlike a lot of things. It is simply hard. I'm not saying that running restaurants isn't difficult, but street food is hard on a different level. Eric decided to move forward with it, and when the time came, some of our team from the Huxley Wallace Collective and I went down and helped him open. We were so honored to be able to assist and be a part of this with and for him.

As we both grew our respective restaurants and restaurant groups over the years, it was evident that Eric was going to be successful in a number of ways. He has a knack for giving people what they want. I say this because a lot of chefs (including myself) have a hard time doing that sometimes. Oftentimes, we give people what we think they should want, and ultimately that either works out or we end up shifting gears and decide to have restaurants that actually sell food. Eric knew this early on, and while he was still introducing his specific point of view and ideas on food, he did it in a way that was approachable and decidedly comforting.

In this business, we, as restaurateurs and chefs, all watch one another. We look at websites, menus, Instagram, and just generally observe how people are doing what they do. I have always looked at Eric, his staff, and how he conducts his business with great admiration. The fact that he's a genuinely good character is a bonus. This business can turn people into assholes pretty quickly, but Eric remains an awesome dude and a good friend. Maybe it's his drawl that lulls me into a sense of ease, but you gotta respect anyone who's able to always push forward in spite of every speed bump that he hits in this business.

I hope, when you read this book, that you realize how special it is to have a restaurant that stays open for more than four or five years. When you add to that the fact that it came from a street food truck, serving a Southern-inspired version of tacos drawn from his Chinese heritage and youth in Japan, you will understand why Eric and his team are unique and why they are so special. The authenticity of his story and his food, his genuine hospitality, and his love of what he does shine bright.

Josh Henderson
Chef & Proprietor, Huxley Wallace Collective

INTRODUCTION

My love of food is why I am here today—the chef-owner of a multifaceted hospitality company that includes three restaurants, two food trucks, a large full-service catering company, and an event space. In 2010, I married my two biggest passions—food and entrepreneurship—and set out on a journey to turn these passions into a profit. My entire life I have never felt that I fit the mold. I spent the better part of my childhood growing up in Japan as a mixed-race kid and then moved to Atlanta at the age of eleven. Most chef-entrepreneurs can't be pigeonholed in a box, and I am no different. For thirty-six years I've embraced the journey but made it a point to only look ahead.

If you leave with just one takeaway from reading this book, I hope it's the realization that life is short. Tomorrow is never guaranteed, and life can be cut short at any moment. I'm a realist, not a philosopher or a scientist. This is how I live my life—like there is no tomorrow. This approach is what forced me to leave my job as a litigator when I was twenty-seven years old to start a food truck. I left behind a six-figure paycheck, insurance, benefits, and friends to pursue a dream, because I felt that time was passing me by. I never wanted to ask "What if?" I never wanted to look back and regret that I never gave my dreams a shot. I never gave a fuck what people thought of me for leaving law to pursue my passion. Maybe I was throwing away my degree, but that still felt better than being miserable, trying to will myself to love the practice of law.

Since 2010, when I opened The Peached Tortilla, fear has been my biggest driver. While I am afraid to fail, the biggest fear I have is of letting myself down. Not giving enough effort. Not being persistent enough. If two people who are equally smart and equally creative start at the same place, the one who puts in more effort usually gets further. Michael Jordan and Kobe Bryant were certainly gifted athletes, but they also outworked all their counterparts. It's no different in the food-truck ecosystem, where thousands of chefs, entrepreneurs, and hobbyists try to transform their passions into legitimate businesses. In the food-truck world, it's all or nothing. To separate yourself from the pack, get noticed, and build profits, you must go from zero to one hundred and never stop.

Fear is what drove me to flip the food-truck model on its head and start a catering company. I didn't want to fail, but nearly a year into the business, I was close to folding. I had made every rookie mistake in the book. I was terrible at managing people and ticket times. I replaced my entire staff three times in one year. Money was flowing the wrong way. After reaching rock-bottom, I decided everyone in the food-truck industry was doing it wrong. We were all staying out until 3:00 a.m. trying to serve the late-night-drunk crowd for pennies on the dollar. I was killing myself selling $2.25 tacos. Instead, I decided I was going to use the food truck for what it was intrinsically—a kitchen on wheels—and sell our brand as a catering company for private events. I hired a sales force, partnered with an events company, and rebranded. I've never looked back.

From the very beginning, my dream was to become a restaurant owner. I tell everyone this: I opened my restaurant out of ego, not out of a desire to get rich. You don't open restaurants to get rich. For me, the restaurant was the end of one journey and the beginning of another, and it symbolized the closing of a chapter I had opened five years earlier. It was proof that you can change your career, pursue your passions, and take a risk. And that it would all be okay.

Much like the company, I did not want the restaurant to fit in a box. We were going to serve comfort food heavily influenced by my youth in Asia and Atlanta. Some plates were going to be a more modern take on these dishes, while others would stay true to the dishes I ate twenty years earlier. The restaurant, for better or worse, was going to be a reflection of me. Dining at the restaurant would give you a glimpse into where I came from, where I am now, and everything in between.

The recipes in this book represent the journey I've been on for over thirty-six years, from Tokyo to Atlanta to Austin. They represent a cultural mishmash, because that is who I am. I am a literal fusion of Chinese, Jewish, and American with a heavy sprinkling of Japanese. Beyond the recipes, I hope you, too, can realize that, much like your approach to cooking, you do not need to live your life in a box. Go out and follow your passions and dreams. Worry less about what other people think and worry more about whether you'll have any regrets. Live your life for *yourself*. It's *your* life. I promise, good things will happen.

Eric Silverstein
Executive Chef and Owner of The Peached Tortilla, Austin, Texas

COOKING NOTES TO GET OUT OF THE WAY

ACHIEVING THE PERFECT CUT & JAPANESE MANDOLINES

When any of the recipes in this book call for julienned onions, shredded cabbage, or thinly sliced radishes, cucumbers, etc., I recommend you use a mandoline. One of the tools we use on a daily basis in our kitchen is a Japanese BENRINER® "little beni" mandoline slicer. These are relatively cheap and can be picked up at any Asian grocery store for about $35. They are usually found in the kitchen tools section. If any of the mandoline's four stainless steel blades gets worn down, you can always purchase replacements online. If you can't find this mandoline at an Asian grocery store, you can search for one on Amazon. You should be just fine with the smaller-width mandoline if you can't find the larger model. Oftentimes, a recipe will not call for the use of a blade insert (i.e., when you are not julienning). It will only call for the use of the flat blade, which is built into the mandoline. I highly recommend purchasing one of these tools; it will save you time and make you look like a pro.

EGGS (SIX-MINUTE VERSUS CIRCULATED EGGS)

I love cooking with eggs—a theme you'll see running through the menus at Peached. I love a good fried egg, and I'm also partial to a slow-poached egg, cooked in a water bath using an immersion circulator. We use an immersion circulator frequently at the restaurant because it allows us to poach eggs ahead of time and then crack them directly onto the plate when we're ready to serve. To get a perfect slow-poached egg with a loose outer white and a runny yolk, you can circulate eggs at 145°F for 45 minutes and then shock them in an ice bath. In Japan, this is known as an *onsen tamago*. If you don't have a circulator, you can always cook a six-minute egg using a boiling pot of hot water. Drop the egg in the boiling water for six minutes, then shock it immediately in an ice bath. I always want loose yolks so I can mix them up with my rice.

FRYING AT HOME

A handful of the recipes in this book call for deep-frying. If high-heat roasting is an option to achieve the Maillard reaction (the chemical reaction that gives browned food its distinctive flavor), I will let you know. But some foods just need to be deep-fried. In that case, you can set up a pot that holds two to three quarts of peanut or vegetable oil. Good pot options for deep-frying include a wok, a cast iron pot, or a Dutch oven. After warming the oil over medium heat, wait for it to reach the specified temperature. The best way to continuously monitor the temperature is to attach a candy thermometer to your pot. If the temperature gets too high, lower the heat, and vice versa.

IMMERSION CIRCULATORS

The use of immersion circulators by home cooks has picked up tenfold over the past few years, as cheaper, more accessible products have hit the market for $300 or less. Immersion circulators allow you to cook sous vide—a temperature-controlled cooking process where different types of food are vacuum-sealed in bags and cooked in a hot-water bath. Immersion circulators are great to have at home, not only because they help lock in flavor and juices but also because they can help take the trial and error out of cooking. An immersion circulator is not necessary for any of the recipes in this book, but you can utilize one where suggested. If you want to purchase an immersion circulator, I would do so online and opt for either the Sansaire® brand or the Joule® by ChefSteps®. A noncommercial vacuum sealer will work just as well for home cooking. You can set up an immersion circulator in any large kitchen vessel. The circulator just needs something to latch onto while it circulates the water.

MINCING GARLIC & GINGER

You wouldn't be cooking Asian food unless you were using of a lot of garlic and ginger. I like to mince garlic by hand, working my knife back and forth over it. I really don't like the taste of the preminced garlic that you can find at grocery stores and would heavily advise against using it. For ginger, I like to use the edge of a spoon to remove the skin. If you're short on time, use a microplane to finely grate ginger and use it in stir-fries. You can always mince garlic and ginger ahead of time and store it in the fridge for one to two days.

RICE

Rice is a definite essential in Asian cuisine, and it is something I cannot live without. Growing up as a kid, I had never seen rice *not* made in an Asian rice cooker. Nearly every household in Japan owns one. While you can cook rice on a stovetop, I recommend using a Japanese rice cooker. Zojirushi®, one of the top rice cooker manufacturers, has a 5½-cup cooker for less than $150, and it will stay with you for a lifetime. When you are ready to cook rice, always remember to wash it first. I give my rice three baths, each time draining the starch. I primarily cook with jasmine rice and Japanese short-grain rice and use a 1:1 ratio of rice to water. When the rice cooker beeps, make sure to let the rice steam for an additional ten minutes. Then fluff the rice, using a rice paddle to help it aerate. Let the rice sit in the cooker for an additional five minutes after you have fluffed it.

Rice cookers are an integral part of the rice equation.

> **Try to find a rice cooker with a "quick" setting. This will allow you to cut down the cooking time to about forty minutes.**

THERMOMETERS

I recommend having both a meat thermometer and a candy thermometer when you are cooking at home. I prefer a digital meat thermometer because it will read the temperature of a protein (like chicken or beef) faster and more accurately than its nondigital counterpart. I also think a candy thermometer is valuable when you are trying to measure the temperature of hot oil. I like to latch the candy thermometer onto the side of the pot I'm using so I can constantly watch the temperature of the oil. Having both kinds of thermometers on hand will make executing the recipes in this book a lot easier.

WHOLE CHICKENS

It's always more economical to buy a whole chicken, rather than buying chicken parts. Three of the recipes in this book—Hainan Chicken & Rice (page 8), Soy Sauce Chicken (page 42), and Umami Fried Chicken (page 68)—call for whole chickens. The Hainan Chicken & Rice, and Soy Sauce Chicken, are cooked whole, then broken down.) If you are uncomfortable breaking down the chicken after it's cooked, you can always ask your butcher to break it down, and then you can cook the chicken according to the recipe. If you break down the chicken at home after cooking, you do not need to debone the thighs and breasts. You can always cut them directly through the bone using a sharp cleaver. This is how you would eat chicken on the streets of Asia.

WOKS, PANS & SKILLETS

Do you need a wok to execute the recipes in this cookbook? The answer is no. A wok and a wok ring are certainly handy things to have in any home kitchen, not only to enhance flavors but also to batch-cook. When woks are paired with high-BTU burners on the streets of Indonesia, the flavors they produce are challenging to replicate. With all that said, you can execute the recipes in this book at home without a wok. I do think there are a few essential types of pans to have on hand in any home kitchen: a cast iron skillet, a carbon-steel French skillet, and a nonstick pan for eggs. Since the majority of the recipes in this book are meant to serve four, it helps to have large pans in your kitchen. Otherwise, you will need to split up the recipe and cook it in rounds.

Breaking down a whole chicken for Soy Sauce Chicken (page 42).

A FEW ASIAN PANTRY STAPLES TO HAVE ON HAND

There are about a dozen Asian products that are repeatedly used in recipes throughout this book. I like to refer to them as the "usual suspects." I have included a full glossary of not-so-intimidating (okay, fine, they might be a little intimidating) Asian foods on page 219. Here's a list of the usual suspects—basic products you'll need to start building your Asian pantry.

- dark soy sauce
- fish sauce
- *gochujang* (Korean red pepper paste)
- hoisin
- mirin
- nori
- oyster sauce
- rice wine vinegar
- soy sauce
- sriracha
- sweet soy sauce
- white pepper

My advice is to one-stop-shop this list and go to an Asian grocery store to pick up all these products. Otherwise you run the risk of having to make multiple grocery stops.

1

STRAY DOGS & HAWKER STANDS

Clockwise from Top Left: My sister and I on one of our family trips to Bali, Indonesia (1993); Enjoying a cup of Ramen at a young age; Japanese pre-school, where I was the only non-Japanese kid. I did, however, speak Japanese; Taking the subway with my dad in Tokyo (1990); Attending professional sumo practice (1994); my sister and I with a family friend.

To understand the food I cook, you have to start at the beginning. I was born in Tokyo to a Chinese-American mother and a Jewish-American father. For the better part of eleven years, Japan and Asia were all I knew. The food, culture, and experiences of Japan were what I was born into. At an early age, I culturally identified with the Japanese. Even though I was an American citizen with American parents living in Japan, I was born in a different country. I was surrounded by Japanese people and customs. By the age of three, I was speaking and holding conversations in Japanese. I was conversing so well, in fact, that my parents felt comfortable sending me to a Japanese preschool, where I was the only non-Japanese kid. Even though I spoke the language, I was ostracized for being different. So my parents made a U-turn and sent me to an international school, St. Mary's, for kindergarten. I realized at an early age that even though I culturally identified with the Japanese at the time, I was definitely *not* Japanese. I wasn't going to be accepted as Japanese. But was I even American? This was some heavy, confusing stuff for a young kid growing up in a foreign country.

While living in Tokyo caused some major cultural confusion, it offered an incredible opportunity to experience a robust, one-of-a-kind food scene. In Japan, I was surrounded by food, and this is where my true love of food began.

The streets of Japan afford a wildly varied smorgasbord. You could often find me following my nose, scanning the scene for the scent of *yaki-imo*, Japanese smoked yam. Instead of ice cream trucks, we had yam trucks, and some old Japanese guy would shout "Yaki-imoooo!" (the *imo* would drag on forever in his old hoarse voice) to passersby eager to get their hands on some delicious smoked yam, fresh off the grill. My mom would take my sister and me on trips down the street to the local Lawson, a Japanese

Opposite: Tokyo, Japan. My birthplace and home for eleven years.

An older Japanese woman running a yaki-imo truck; I used to chase down these trucks as a kid. My mom would give my sister and me 200 yen so we could buy the treats on the street outside our house.

convenience store, to eat *oden*, a Japanese soup bowl containing anything from boiled eggs and daikon to fish cakes and even octopus, all swirling in a light broth. I also loved to eat *onigiri*, little triangles of seaweed, rice, and a filling. When I was a kid, my mom would always pack some for my lunch or have them on hand for a snack. My favorite onigiri was tuna with mayo: I'd take out the seaweed and wrap the rice with it. Even though I wasn't Japanese, I wanted to eat and experience food like the Japanese.

My favorite food to eat as a kid, though, was, hands-down, *yakitori*—chicken skewers bathed in *tare*, a sweet chicken infused soy sauce. All kinds, including *tsukune* (ground chicken with *shiso* dipped in raw egg), chicken wings, chicken and scallions, etc. We'd walk out of a department store and there would be some random Japanese guy on the street (not to be confused with the yam guy) selling yakitori for 100 yen (about $1 back then)

Onigiri at a Lawson; some of the best snacks and food in the world are sold in these convenience stores.

per skewer. I still remember the first time I ate yakitori—the hot, but not piping-hot, feel of the smoky protein on my tongue and the slightly caramelized glaze of *tare* touching my lips. It was beyond fantastic, and I was quickly addicted, eating yakitori as many times a week as I could get away with.

My parents used to take us to a little yakitori joint in Roppongi, Tokyo, called Nanbantei. It had about thirty-five seats and had served a few former US presidents. There wasn't much cooking equipment there—just the *binchotan* grill for yakitori and a small exhaust hood. About twenty-two years later, I returned to Nanbantei on my honeymoon, and the same *obaasan* (Japanese grandmother) who had served my family when I was a kid greeted and invited me and my wife Kristine to sit at the chef's counter. I'm not sure if I was more in awe of the food or the accomplishment of running a restaurant for that long.

My culinary experiences, as a kid, extended beyond Japanese and Chinese food. For Christmas and summer breaks, my parents would almost always take my sister and me on a family vacation to another Asian country. It was during multiple such trips to Singapore that I was exposed to Malaysian cuisine. My parents would always take us to feast on chicken and rice, *char kway teow* and laksa at the hawker stands. And for at least one night on each trip, we would visit a super-dive restaurant in an area called Punggol, where a stray dog would stare me in the face three feet from our table as I chowed down on some of the best food of my life. The chili crab would arrive piping-hot, the steam rolling right off the top as if from a volcano. We'd tear into the crab with our hands and then move onto the gigantic prawns, which were served heads and tails. To this day, I am not interested in fine dining, mainly because I enjoyed such delicious food in the most unassuming of environments at an early age.

Opposite Top: Lawson was a frequent pit stop for my sister and me after school, especially on colder days. We would load up a bowl of broth with all types of goodies.
Opposite bottom: A yakitori house in Japan; chicken skewers and cold beer.

HAINAN CHICKEN & RICE

Serves 3-4

Hainan Chicken & Rice is one of those dishes that people either *get* or don't get. If you grew up eating the dish, it's pure comfort food. I used to eat it all the time as a kid when my family went on vacation to Singapore. It's hawker-stand food, enjoyed on a melamine plate in 90°F heat and 100 percent humidity. If you've ever been to a hawker stand, then you understand what I'm talking about. It's never about the atmosphere and always about the food. Hainan chicken is served at room temperature with the skin on. The skin is gelatinous, since the chicken is shocked in ice water right after it's done poaching. The flavor of the chicken is subtle, so we help accentuate this with sweet soy sauce, Ginger-Scallion Sauce (page 170), and a little bit of Sambal Oelek chili paste. This is how Singaporeans eat the dish.

FOR THE CHICKEN

1 whole chicken (approximately 3-4 pounds)

Kosher salt, to season the chicken

White pepper, to season the chicken

1½ tablespoons vegetable oil

2-inch knob of ginger, sliced into ¼-inch pieces and smashed

10 cloves garlic

2 stalks of lemongrass, cut into thirds, peeled and smashed

1 yellow onion, peeled and quartered

½ cup soy sauce

3 tablespoons Fish Sauce (see Asian Food Glossary, page 219)

TO MAKE THE CHICKEN

1. Season the chicken with the salt and white pepper on both sides.

2. Place the oil in a large stockpot and set it over medium heat. When the oil starts to shimmer, add the ginger, garlic, lemongrass, and yellow onions to the stockpot, and sauté them until they are aromatic (about 3-4 minutes). Make sure to constantly move the ingredients around the pot so they don't overbrown.

3. Once the ginger, garlic, lemongrass, and yellow onions are aromatic, fill the stockpot halfway with water and add the soy sauce. The heat should still be on medium. Once the liquid in the stockpot begins to boil, lower the heat so that the poaching liquid simmers, and then add the chicken.

4. Simmer the chicken for about 10 minutes per pound. This should be the absolute lightest simmer possible (basically a bare simmer). Simmer until cooked. Use a meat thermometer to check that the chicken reaches an internal temperature of 165°F (this will take about 30 minutes for a 3-pound chicken). Stick a meat thermometer deep inside the chicken breast to take the temperature. If it has still not reached the desired temperature, turn off the heat, cover the stockpot, and let the chicken finish cooking in the already-hot poaching liquid.

5. Once the chicken has reached 165°F, take it out and shock it in a bath of ice water.

This can be in a mixing bowl or a separate stockpot filled with ice water. Once the exterior skin of the chicken has tightened, remove the chicken from the ice bath and set it aside. Pat the chicken dry.

6. Strain the broth remaining in the stockpot. Pour 2½ cups of the strained broth into a medium-size saucepot. Add the fish sauce to the strained broth and reduce it for 3–4 minutes over a rolling boil, over high heat, until it is a little more concentrated. You will use this broth to cook the rice.

> For this recipe you are only keeping 2½ cups of the strained broth. You can either discard the remaining broth or freeze it in an airtight container. If you decide to store the broth, you can use it for the Mapo Tofu Mazemen recipe on page 148. The broth will keep for 2–3 months in your freezer.

7. Cut the chicken into serving pieces (see notes, page xvii).

FOR THE RICE

Makes 4 cups

2 cups jasmine rice, raw
2 cups chicken broth

TO MAKE THE RICE

Cover the rice with cold water while it is in the rice-cooker pot. Rinse the rice and then strain, discarding the cloudy white water. Repeat this process 3 times.

After discarding all the water, pour the 2 cups of reserved chicken broth into the rice-cooker pot.

Set the rice cooker on cook. When the rice is done, let it sit and steam, covered, for 10 minutes in the rice cooker. After 10 minutes, open the rice cooker and aerate the rice by lifting a little bit of rice at a time with the paddle, allowing air to get between the grains. Repeat this process 3–4 times, each time lifting and separating the rice, until you have made your way to the bottom of the rice cooker.

ASSEMBLY

½ English (seedless) cucumber

¼ cup Sweet Soy Sauce (see Asian Food Glossary, page 219)

Cilantro leaves, for garnish

¼ cup or more Ginger-Scallion Sauce (page 170)

¼ cup Sambal Oelek chili paste (see Asian Food Glossary, page 219)

1. Using a vegetable peeler, peel the skin of the cucumber lengthwise, leaving a gap between the peeled areas to create a striped appearance. Slice the cucumber widthwise into ¼-inch medallions.

2. Drizzle the sweet soy sauce over the chicken. Top it with cilantro leaves.

Serve the chicken with a side of rice, the cucumbers, Ginger-Scallion Sauce, and sambal chili paste.

> Hawker stands are small-footprint, open-air food stalls, typically found in Singapore and Indonesia. They are clustered with other hawker stands and share a common seating area. Think food halls without air-conditioning and modern-day architecture.

CHAR KWAY TEOW

Serves 4

Char kway teow, which translates to "stir-fried rice cake strips," is another hawker-stand dish that has a heavy Malaysian influence. It's very popular in Singapore and certain parts of Malaysia. Traditionally, this dish is made with cockles and served with the head-on prawns. I have modified the dish a bit (since it's not easy to find cockles), while still staying true to its street-food roots.

FOR THE SAUCE

1 tablespoon Shrimp Paste
  (see Asian Food Glossary, page 219)

2¼ tablespoons light soy sauce

1 tablespoon Sweet Soy Sauce
  (see Asian Food Glossary, page 219)

2¼ tablespoons Oyster Sauce
  (see Asian Food Glossary, page 219)

3¼ tablespoons Chili Garlic Sauce
  (see Asian Food Glossary, page 219)

TO MAKE THE SAUCE

Place all the ingredients in a small bowl and mix them together with a spoon. Set the bowl aside.

FOR THE NOODLES

2 tablespoons vegetable oil

2 cloves garlic, minced

¼ inch slice ginger, minced

¾ pound Lap Cheong (Chinese sausage)
(see Asian Food Glossary, page 219)

¼ pound deep-fried Fish Cakes
(see Asian Food Glossary, page 219)

½ pound large shrimp, tail on, peeled
and deveined

3 eggs, cracked and whisked together

1½ pounds ho fun noodles, peeled
(see Note)

Pinch of white pepper

1 cup Chinese chives, cut into 3-inch pieces

1½ cup bean sprouts

¼ cup cilantro, for garnish

Note Ho fun noodles, which are sold fresh, need to be hand-peeled. Make sure to purchase noodles that are precut. If the noodles sit on the shelf for a while, you'll need to heat the packet before you pull the noodles apart; otherwise it will be difficult to separate them. I recommend taking the noodles out of the package and microwaving them for 20 seconds to loosen them prior to peeling.

TO MAKE THE NOODLES

1. Heat a wok or a wide nonstick stir-fry pan over medium-low heat and add 1 tablespoon of the oil. Wait for the oil to shimmer and then add the garlic and ginger. If the garlic starts to burn, reduce the heat.

2. Once the garlic and ginger are fragrant, add the lap cheong and fish cakes. Stir-fry them until they begin to take on a little bit of color and cook through. This should take about 45 seconds. Add the shrimp to the pan and continue to cook all the ingredients for another 30 seconds.

3. Move all the ingredients to one side of the pan, then pour the remaining tablespoon of oil on the other, empty side of the pan. Pour the eggs into the empty side and scramble them. Once they are cooked all the way through after 1 minute, incorporate the eggs into the Lap Cheong, fish cakes, and shrimp. The idea is not to cook the shrimp all the way through before you add the ho fun noodles. The shrimp will continue to cook in the pan until the dish is ready to serve.

4. Add the ho fun noodles to the pan and begin to stir the noodles over medium-high heat. Make sure to constantly turn the noodles when you stir-fry them so they don't stick to the bottom of the pan and burn. Don't be overly aggressive with the noodles, however, or they will break.

5. Once the noodles have cooked for 1 minute, add the sauce and a pinch of white pepper. Continue to stir-fry the noodles for another 2¹⁄₂–3 minutes.

6. Taste the noodles to make sure they are getting close to al dente. Add the Chinese chives and bean sprouts and stir-fry the noodles for another 30 seconds.

7. Take the noodles off the heat and plate them. Garnish the noodles with the cilantro.

> **If your wok or pan is not big enough, you may need to cook this dish in multiple rounds. That's fine. You can always cut your ingredients in half and repeat the process.**

BACON & SHRIMP OKONOMIYAKI

Serves 4 (½ pancake per serving)

Okonomiyaki brings back memories of cooking tableside in Japan, where okonomiyaki restaurants typically have a flat-top grill installed right in the table. The server ladles the batter onto the center of the grill, and you can watch the pancake cook as it sizzles at the table. Servers flip the pancake for you, and then top it with okonomiyaki sauce and kewpie mayo. You can then throw on additional toppings like bonito, aonori, togarashi, beni shoga, and anything else your mind can dream up.

Note *There is no rule that you have to use bacon and shrimp in this recipe. You can always sub in other ingredients, like squid or octopus. One other option is to use yakisoba as a base for the okonomiyaki. In that scenario, you would stir-fry some yakisoba noodles with some yakisoba seasoning or okonomiyaki sauce. Then, ladle the batter directly on top of the yakisoba noodles.*

FOR THE BATTER

1⅓ cups all-purpose flour

⅓ cup plus 2 tablespoons Dashi (page 167)

⅓ teaspoon salt

2 eggs, beaten

⅓ cup nagaimo (Japanese yam, grated)

2 cups green cabbage, shredded

TO MAKE THE BATTER

1. In a mixing bowl, whisk the flour, dashi, and salt. Whisk the eggs and nagaimo into the flour mixture until the ingredients are fully incorporated.

2. Mix the cabbage into the batter.

FOR THE PANCAKES

2 tablespoons vegetable oil

6 ounces shrimp (about 4 large shrimp), peeled, deveined, and diced

3 ounces thick-cut bacon, fried and chopped into ½-inch pieces

⅓ cup Okonomiyaki Sauce (see Asian Food Glossary, page 219)

¼ cup Kewpie Mayo (see Asian Food Glossary, page 219)

¼ cup Bonito Flakes (see Asian Food Glossary, page 219), for garnish

2 tablespoons Aonori (see Asian Food Glossary, page 219), for garnish

TO MAKE THE PANCAKES

1. In a deep 8-inch-wide carbon-steel or cast iron skillet, heat 1 tablespoon of the oil over medium-low heat. Add the shrimp to the pan and sauté. Once the shrimp is cooked about three-quarters of the way through, remove half of it and set that aside. You will make the pancakes in two rounds.

. . . .

Note If you don't have an 8-inch skillet, you can always cook the pancakes in a larger pan. Just make sure the batter doesn't run very far or you will have a very thin pancake.

. . . .

2. Add 1½ ounces of the chopped bacon to the pan with the shrimp. Ladle 1½ cups of the okonomiyaki batter over the shrimp and bacon. Cook the mixture over medium-low heat for 3–4 minutes. Once the bottom has browned, flip the pancake.

3. Cook the pancake for another 3–4 minutes until it is done. Gently press the top of the pancake to see if it is very soft or a little bit hard. It should not be so soft that you can pierce it with your finger. You can always stick a knife through the pancake to see if any batter sticks to it. If none of the batter sticks to the knife, it is done. Repeat this process with the remaining bacon, shrimp, and okonomiyaki batter.

4. Top the okonomiyaki with a healthy amount of okonomiyaki sauce, kewpie mayo, bonito flakes, and aonori. You can use a squeeze bottle for the okonomiyaki sauce and kewpie mayo to cover the pancake and make it look just like the Japanese do!

LAKSA

Serves 4

For some reason, laksa has yet to make its way into the mainstream, maybe because it's a Malaysian dish, and Malaysian cuisine isn't as popular in the United States as Japanese, Chinese, or Korean food. It could also be due to the fact that laksa has a prawn- or shrimp-based broth, as opposed to a chicken or pork broth. Regardless, it is the perfect dish to devour on a cold winter night or a rainy night. The broth is rich and coats the noodles perfectly. If you are into seafood, this is the dish for you.

> The recipes for shrimp stock and laksa paste will yield slightly more laksa broth than you will need to serve four people. However, the broth will last in the refrigerator for four to five days, so you can always make the dish again the same week.

FOR THE SHRIMP STOCK

Makes 6 cups

5 cups shrimp shells (about 1¼ pounds), washed

½ tablespoon unsalted butter

3 cloves garlic, peeled

½ yellow onion, quartered

> Shrimp shells may be difficult to find. Your best bet would be to go to your local seafood shop or the seafood counter at the supermarket and ask if they have either shrimp shells or shrimp heads on hand.

TO MAKE THE SHRIMP STOCK

1. Preheat the oven to 350°F. When the oven is at temperature, roast the shrimp shells on a baking sheet for 30 minutes.

2. In a medium-size stockpot, melt the butter over low heat.

3. Once the butter has melted, add the garlic and onion to the pan and sauté them over medium-low heat for 2–3 minutes.

4. Once the garlic and onions have become aromatic and lightly browned, add the shrimp shells and continue to sauté the mixture.

5. After 2 minutes of continuous stirring, add 9 cups of water to the stockpot. Simmer all the ingredients over low heat for 90 minutes, making sure to skim the foam off the top of the stock from time to time.

6. Strain the stock with a fine-mesh strainer and set it aside.

FOR THE LAKSA PASTE

Makes 1 ⅓ cups

2 dried Thai Chilies (see Asian Food Glossary, page 219)

3 tablespoons toasted peanuts

1 teaspoon ginger, grated

6 cloves garlic, peeled

¼ cup mint leaves

1½ ounces fresh turmeric, peeled and roughly chopped

1½ tablespoons Shrimp Paste (see Asian Food Glossary, page 219)

1½ ounces serrano peppers, seeded and tops removed, roughly chopped

¼ teaspoon lime zest

½ cup lemongrass, roughly chopped (outer shell removed; from about 2 lemongrass stalks)

¼ red onion, peeled and roughly chopped

¼ yellow onion, peeled and roughly chopped

TO MAKE THE LAKSA PASTE

1. Soak the dried Thai chilies in hot water for 5 minutes, then drain them.

2. Soak the toasted peanuts in hot water for 10 minutes, then drain them.

3. Blend the Thai chilies, peanuts, and the remaining ingredients together in a food processor until a yellowish-orange paste forms.

FOR THE LAKSA BROTH

Makes about 8 cups

1 tablespoon vegetable oil

1⅓ cups Laksa Paste (recipe above)

6 cups shrimp stock

2 cups coconut milk

2 tablespoons + 1 teaspoon Fish Sauce
  (see Asian Food Glossary, page 219)

2 tablespoons + 1 teaspoon brown sugar

Juice of 1 lime

TO MAKE THE LAKSA BROTH

1. Heat the oil in a medium-size stockpot over medium-low heat.

2. Once the oil starts to shimmer, add the laksa paste and cook for 5 minutes. Frequently stir the paste as it cooks.

3. Add the shrimp stock, coconut milk, fish sauce, brown sugar, and lime juice into the stockpot and continue to heat everything until the laksa broth has reached a simmer.

ASSEMBLY

4 (6-ounce) portions Tonkotsu ramen
  noodles or 24 ounces Pancit Canton
  Noodles (see Noodle Glossary, page 216)

6 cups Laksa Broth (recipe above)

1 pound shrimp, tails on, peeled and deveined

Four 6-minute eggs, or onsen tamagos
  (see Cooking Notes, page xv)

2 cups bean sprouts

½ cup green onions, chopped

GARNISHES

½ cup mint leaves

½ cup cilantro leaves

½ cup Thai basil leaves

½ lime, quartered into wedges

Togarashi (see Asian Food Glossary, page 219)
  (optional)

Aonori (see Asian Food Glossary, page 219)
  (optional)

4 teaspoons Sambal Oelek chili paste
  (see Asian Food Glossary, page 219) (optional)

1 teaspoon Chili Garlic Sauce
  (see Asian Food Glossary, page 219) (optional)

1. Heat 3 quarts of water in a medium-size pot over high heat until it boils.

2. When the water comes to a boil, drop the noodles into the pot and cook them according to the directions on the package.

3. While the noodles are cooking, heat the laksa broth in a medium saucepot over medium heat.

4. When the broth starts to simmer, poach the shrimp in the laksa broth. This should take about 3 minutes on one side and another 2 minutes on the other.

5. After the noodles are done cooking, divide them evenly among separate bowls. Top the noodles with an even amount of the laksa broth.

6. Top the noodles in each bowl with the poached shrimp, eggs, bean sprouts, green onions, herbs, and a lime wedge. If you like, continue to garnish the laksa with a sprinkle of togarashi and aonori, along with a teaspoon of chili garlic sauce.

#60 FRIED RICE

Serves 4

Making good fried rice is almost like a rite of passage if you're Chinese. The great thing about cooking a lot of rice at home is you are bound to have some left over. There's an ongoing debate as to whether or not day-old rice makes fried rice better. I tend to think it does, mainly because a lot of the surface moisture evaporates from the rice overnight and your fried rice ends up sticking together less. If you are going to fry day-old rice, you will need to make it the day before, and then refrigerate it, loosely covered, overnight. To me there's no real right or wrong, in terms of the vegetables and proteins you can add to fried rice. However, I do think there's a process to follow and certain key ingredients to include. Depending on the size of the pan you're using, you may need to split this recipe in two.

4 tablespoons vegetable oil

2 cloves garlic, minced

¼-inch knob peeled ginger, minced on a microplane (about 2 teaspoons)

½ pound Lap Cheong (Chinese sausage) (see Asian Food Glossary, page 219)

1¼ cups shiitake mushrooms, stems removed, cleaned and sliced

½ cup green onions, chopped

2 eggs, beaten

2 heavy pinches white pepper

4 cups cold, day-old jasmine rice (already cooked)

1½ tablespoons butter

1 teaspoon Shiro Miso (see Asian Food Glossary, page 219)

3 tablespoons Oyster Sauce (see Asian Food Glossary, page 219)

Cilantro, for garnish

1 cup rice puffs (from 1 rice paper wrapper) (optional) (see Note)

¼ cup Peach Pickled Red Onions (page 179) or julienned red onions

Note *Rice puffs are simple to make and give a great texture to a lot of dishes. Heat 2 quarts of oil in a pot to 350°F. Then, gently place the rice paper wrappers into the oil. The rice papers should immediately puff up and you should really be able to smell the fried rice paper. Immediately remove the rice puffs with a spider or a slotted stainless steel spoon and set them on a plate covered with a paper towel. The rice papers should only fry for 10 seconds. Once the rice puffs have cooled, break them up with your hands into ½ × ½-inch pieces.*

1. In a wok or a large pan, heat 3 tablespoons of the oil over low heat. When the oil starts to shimmer, add the garlic and ginger.

2. When the garlic and ginger have become aromatic, add the lap cheong, shiitake mushrooms, and green onions. Continue to stir-fry all the ingredients over medium heat for 3 minutes.

3. Move the lap cheong mixture to a separate plate. Heat 1 tablespoon of the oil in the empty pan over medium-low heat. Add the beaten eggs and scramble them. Season the eggs with a heavy pinch of white pepper.

> **It's really important to create a layer of oil in the pan, between the pan itself and the eggs. This will prevent the eggs from sticking to the pan. When you add the 1 tablespoon of vegetable oil to the empty pan, make sure it spreads over the bottom of the pan, and then pour the beaten eggs directly on top of the oil.**

4. Once the scrambled eggs are cooked, place the lap cheong mixture back into the pan. Add the 4 cups of cold rice and increase the heat to high.

5. Add the butter, shiro miso, oyster sauce, and a heavy pinch of white pepper to the pan. Stir-fry the mixture over medium-high heat for 3–4 minutes, making sure to incorporate all the ingredients.

6. Place the fried rice on a big serving platter, and top the rice with cilantro, rice puffs, and peach pickled red onions.

Serves 3-4

The ultimate Hawaiian-inspired brunch dish, this is the type of meal you want to dive into after a heavy night of drinking (assuming you can stand up and cook). SPAM can sometimes be off-putting to people, but the Koreans continue to use it in their Army stew (*Budae Jjigae*), and the Hawaiians are still very fond of it, too (think SPAM Musubi). It packs a salty umami punch that is tough to replicate.

2 tablespoons vegetable oil

2 cloves garlic, minced

¾ teaspoon ginger, minced

4 eggs, 2 of which have been beaten in a separate bowl and the other 2 left whole

Pinch of kosher salt

Pinch of freshly ground black pepper

½ pound SPAM, diced into ¼ × ¼-inch pieces

1¼ cups shiitake mushrooms, stems removed, cleaned and sliced

¾ cup green onions, chopped

2 heavy pinches white pepper

4 cups cold cooked, day-old jasmine rice (see sidebar, page 20)

1½ tablespoons butter

3 tablespoons Kimchi (page 173) or use store-bought, pureed

½ teaspoon Shiro Miso (see Asian Food Glossary, page 219)

3 tablespoons Oyster Sauce (see Asian Food Glossary, page 219)

2 tablespoons Dehydrated Egg Furikake (see Asian Food Glossary, page 219) (or substitute with Aonori)

2½ tablespoons Fried Shallots (see Asian Food Glossary, page 219)

1. Heat ½ tablespoon of the oil in a wok or a large pan over low heat. When the oil starts to shimmer, add the garlic and ginger to the pan.

> If you only have one wok or pan, you may need to split the ingredients in half and cook them separately, since this recipe serves 3–4.

2. Heat 1 tablespoon of the oil in a separate nonstick pan over low heat. Add the 2 unbeaten eggs to the pan and cook them sunny side up. Season the eggs with a pinch of salt and a pinch of freshly ground black pepper.

3. When the garlic and ginger have become aromatic after 30 seconds, add the SPAM, shiitake mushrooms, and ½ cup of green onions. Stir-fry the ingredients over medium heat.

4. Remove the SPAM mixture from the heat and transfer it to a plate. Set it aside. Add ½ tablespoon of oil to the same pan over medium-low heat. Then add the beaten eggs and scramble them. Season the scrambled eggs with a heavy pinch of white pepper.

5. Once the scrambled eggs are cooked, add the SPAM, shiitake mushrooms, and green onions back into the pan. Add the 4 cups of cold, precooked rice to the pan and increase the heat to high.

6. Add the butter, kimchi puree, shiro miso, oyster sauce, and heavy pinch of white pepper. Continue to stir-fry the mixture over high heat for 3–4 minutes, making sure to incorporate all the ingredients.

7. To plate the dish, spoon the fried rice onto a big serving platter and top it with the 2 fried eggs. Scatter the remaining ¼ cup of green onions, dehydrated egg furikake, and fried shallots over the fried rice and eggs.

A lot of people get hung up on timing fried eggs so that they're ready exactly when the dish is ready. It's completely fine if you finish your eggs ahead of time— just take them out of the pan and put them on a plate in a hot spot in your kitchen; for instance, the area right next to the burners you're using to cook the dish. Alternatively, you can always finish making the fried rice (which will stay hot in the pan you are using for 5 minutes) and *then* cook the eggs. Either method works to ensure that you have a hot plate of fried rice and fried eggs.

LOCO MY MOCO

Serves 4

The loco moco, one of Hawaii's staple dishes, is still a relative unknown outside of Hawaii and the West Coast. It's something I can imagine Hawaiians waking up to, and filling their stomachs with, before hitting the beach for a morning surf. It's basic in the sense that the main elements are a hamburger and a fried egg. However, I kick it up a notch with a dashi gravy that really adds a layer of flavor to the overall dish. You can make the dashi and onion jam or caramelized onions the day before, and focus on the rest of the dish when you get up to make it for breakfast or brunch.

FOR THE DASHI GRAVY

4 tablespoons unsalted butter

¼ cup + 2 tablespoons flour

2 cups Dashi (page 167)

¼ cup beef broth

2½ tablespoons heavy cream

¼ teaspoon white pepper

TO MAKE THE DASHI GRAVY

1. Melt the butter in a small saucepan over medium-low heat. Once the butter is melted, slowly whisk in the flour to make a roux.

2. Reduce the heat to low, and continue to stir and cook the the roux until it turns brown. When the roux is cooked it will have a nutty aroma. This should take 7–8 minutes.

3. In a separate saucepot, heat the dashi and beef broth over medium heat.

4. Add the cream to the cooked roux and continue to whisk the mixture over medium heat. Taste the roux and make sure there is no taste of flour on your tongue. This is important, as you don't want the taste of the flour to make its way into the gravy.

5. Slowly add the hot dashi and beef broth to the roux.

6. Add the white pepper to the gravy. Keeping the heat on medium-low, whisk the gravy frequently until it thickens. It should thicken in 3–4 minutes. Keep the gravy covered hot, over low heat, until you are ready to serve it.

ASSEMBLY

2 tablespoons vegetable oil

4 (4-ounce) hamburger patties

Pinch of kosher salt

Pinch of freshly ground black pepper

4 eggs

2 cups jasmine rice, cooked

4 tablespoons Onion Jam (page 81), heated, or Miso Caramelized Onions (page 64) (see Note)

¾ cup green onions, chopped

Fried Shallots (see Asian Food Glossary, page 219), for garnish

Togarashi (see Asian Food Glossary, page 219), for garnish

Note Onion Jam and/or Miso Caramelized Onions are not necessary for this dish, if you don't have the time to prep them. The dish will taste just as good without them, although the sweetness of the onions does add another dimension to the overall dish.

1. Heat a large skillet over medium-high heat and add 1 tablespoon of the oil. Season the hamburger patties with salt and pepper. Once the oil starts to shimmer, place the hamburger patties in the skillet. You may need to do this in two separate pans simultaneously. Alternatively, you can do this in rounds, in the same pan.

2. When you start to see the blood run through the meat, flip the patties. For a medium cook on the burgers, you will need to fry them another 2 minutes before taking them off the heat.

3. In a separate pan, using the remaining 1 tablespoon of oil, cook the eggs, sunny side up, over low heat. Season them with salt and pepper. It's very important to control the heat when cooking eggs. If the heat is too high, you will overcook the bottom of the eggs and they will be rubbery.

4. Spoon ½ cup of cooked rice onto the bottom of a plate. Spread the rice out so that it isn't a mound. Place a tablespoon of the Onion Jam or Miso Caramelized Onions on top of the rice.

5. Lay the cooked burger patty on top of the rice, and then place a fried egg on top of the burger patty. Using a large spoon or a ladle, spoon some of the dashi gravy on top of the egg and burger patty, leaving the yolk exposed.

6. Garnish the dish with green onions, fried shallots, and a pinch of Togarashi.

AHI TUNA POKE BOWL

Serves 3–4

Starting in 2014–2015, Poke hit the gas pedal and entered the consciousness of mainstream America in a big way. Since then, the trend has really taken off. What I love about poke is that it's fresh, easy to prep, and filling. I think the Hawaiians have been onto something for a while. This is a recipe from Peached's former culinary director, now catering director, Stephani O'Connor. Stephani, a super-talented chef, came up with this recipe before we opened up for lunch at the restaurant.

FOR THE POKE DRESSING

½ cup soy sauce

2 teaspoons rice vinegar

1 tablespoon sesame oil

½ tablespoon red pepper flakes

2 tablespoons green onion, thinly sliced widthwise

½ teaspoon white sesame seeds, toasted

1 tablespoon sugar

1 tablespoon lime juice

This recipe yields more dressing than you will need for the dish. The remaining dressing will hold up for two weeks in the refrigerator. You can always use the extra dressing as a dipping sauce for dumplings and Korean-style savory pancakes (*pajeon*).

TO MAKE THE POKE DRESSING

Place all the ingredients in a small saucepan over low heat. Once the sugar has melted and dissolved into the dressing, remove the saucepan from the heat and pour the dressing into a heat-proof bowl. Place the bowl, uncovered, in the refrigerator so that it can cool immediately.

ASSEMBLY

1 pound ahi tuna (sinew removed), cut into ¼ × ¼-inch cubes

½ cup Poke Dressing (recipe above)

1½ cups Japanese short-grain rice (3 cups cooked)

1½ cups green cabbage, shredded thinly on a mandoline

⅓ cup English (seedless) cucumber, thinly sliced to ⅛ inch on a mandoline (about ¼ of a cucumber)

1 avocado, peeled, pitted, and sliced

⅓ cup green onions, chopped

1½ tablespoons Dehydrated Egg Furikake (see "Furikake" in the Asian Food Glossary, page 219)

¼ cup Wasabi Mayo (page 186)

½ lime, cut into wedges

3 sprigs cilantro, for garnish

1. In a large mixing bowl, toss the ahi tuna with the poke dressing.

2. Place about ¾ cup of the cooked rice into the bottom of three or four bowls.

3. Top the rice with a little bit of green cabbage to cover it, then top the cabbage with a portion of the dressed tuna (a little less than ¼ cup). Make sure to pour some of the dressing from the bowl on top of the cabbage.

4. Top each bowl with cucumber slices and avocado.

5. Sprinkle the green onions and dried egg furikake over the bowls, and then spoon the wasabi aioli on top.

6. Garnish each dish with a lime wedge and cilantro.

JAPANESE STREET CORN

Serves 4

Elotes, grilled Mexican street corn, are wildly popular in certain parts of the United States (and, of course, in Mexico itself). This is my version, bringing Japanese ingredients to the familiar street corn dish.

¼ cup Cotija cheese, grated

4 large ears yellow or white corn, husks removed and cleaned

1 tablespoon vegetable oil

¼ cup Kewpie Mayo (see Asian Food Glossary, page 219)

1½ teaspoons Aonori (see Asian Food Glossary, page 219)

1½ teaspoons Togarashi (see Asian Food Glossary, page 219)

1 cup Bonito Flakes (see Asian Food Glossary, page 219)

A lot of Japanese chefs shave their own bonito, right before service, with a bonito box. These little wooden boxes can be purchased online and are imported directly from Japan. They function like a mandoline, except there is only one blade, and the bonito shavings are caught in a drawer that pulls out of the box. Freshly shaved bonito has a pronounced, fishy flavor that adds an extra layer of umami to dishes. You can also purchase whole dried bonito online through Amazon or at specialty Asian retailers.

Shaving dried bonito into a traditional Japanese box.

1. Spread the Cotija over a large plate.

2. Heat a grill pan over medium heat and brush the corn with the oil (see Note).

- -

Note If you don't have a grill pan, you can always cook the corn in the oven at 350°F. Just set the corn cobs, with the husks on, directly on an oven rack and bake them for 25–30 minutes.

- -

3. When the pan is hot, place the ears of corn in the pan and give the corn nice grill marks.

4. After 2–3 minutes, when you start to see dark grill marks appear on the corn, rotate the corn. Continue to rotate the corn until grill marks appear on every side. The corn should take about 8–10 minutes to cook. Once the corn is done, remove the ears from the pan.

5. Using an offset spatula or a knife, coat the exterior of each piece of corn with the kewpie mayo.

6. Once each ear of corn is coated with mayo, roll it in the Cotija.

7. To finish garnishing the corn, sprinkle the aonori, togarashi, and bonito flakes on top.

2

MOM'S CHINESE HOME COOKING

Opposite: Cooking at home is always fun, because home is where my heart is.

At home, my mom was always cooking for our family. We rarely missed dinner together. I'm convinced that my love of food has been largely influenced by attributing positive memories to it. Growing up, I was able to share food with the people I loved most—my family. My mom cooked a lot of Chinese food for us—making *chow fun*, soy sauce chicken, congee, and all sorts of comfort food that she'd grown up on. When I wasn't eating Japanese street food, I was eating my mom's Chinese food. It's a miracle I stayed a skinny kid.

Oftentimes, my mom would help my sister and me with homework when we got home. We would do our homework on a long wooden dining table in the kitchen. My mom would start prepping dinner around 5:00 or 5:30 p.m., as we were finishing our homework. The intoxicating aroma of ginger, garlic, and onions would start to permeate our work area. Once my sister and I finished, we would hurry up and clear the table so we could help out our mom. On *gyoza* (the Japanese term for dumplings) nights, we would help her roll pork-and-cabbage filling into dumpling wrappers. She would always demonstrate the first one, ever-so-gently placing a small dollop of pork mixture into the center of the wrapper and then dabbing her finger in a little bit of water to seal the ends. Then she would fold, fold, fold. My sister and I were in awe of how fast our mom made dumplings. We were always laboring behind, usually putting too much filling in the wrapper.

We didn't always eat Chinese food at home. My mom would sometimes set up a gas burner in the middle of the table with a pot of hot broth, and we would eat *shabu shabu* (Japanese hot pot). She would have plates of vegetables (enoki mushrooms, Napa cabbage, tofu), proteins (thinly sliced beef), udon noodles, and, of course, shabu sauce. It was a tradition to save the udon noodles for last. Served with the pot broth and topped with a little bit of white pepper and togarashi, they were my favorite part of the meal. *That* is what family dinner was all about. We were all able to cook our own meals at the table over good conversation.

Above: Cooking dumplings with my sister.
Opposite: My childhood home in Setagaya, Tokyo, Japan.

SOUTHERN FUN NOODLES

Serves 4

Chow fun is one of the dishes that defined my childhood. It was my favorite growing up, and whenever my mom told me chow fun was for dinner, my eyes would light up. Nowadays, when I go home to Las Vegas—where my parents currently live—for Thanksgiving or Christmas, it's the first thing waiting for me at the dinner table when I walk in the door.

My mom's chow fun is a little different than the dish we serve at the restaurant. I would call hers a more traditional version. It's also a little lower in sodium. In more recent years, my mom has cooked with less oyster sauce and soy sauce. Personally, I'm okay with using those ingredients. I'm not one to walk away from MSG. I eat because I enjoy eating and I enjoy food. If I'm going to take the time to make a dish, I want it to be flavorful and robust.

While our rendition of chow fun, called Southern Fun, uses a lot of the traditional ingredients—garlic, ginger, onions, bean sprouts, and ho fun rice noodles—we tweak the dish just enough to make it distinctive and ours. In true Austin fashion, we use brisket as the protein component in the dish. For typical chow fun, you're looking at some form of low-cut red meat thinly sliced and marinated in a little bit of soy, sugar, cornstarch, white pepper, and Chinese cooking wine.

I really think, however, that our secret is in the sauce. We use a blend of regular soy, chili-garlic sauce, sweet soy, and oyster sauce. Sweet soy is one of the most magical Asian ingredients I have ever cooked with. It almost has the consistency of molasses, with a licorice back-end taste to it. Sweet soy really lights up this dish, and contrasts perfectly with the regular soy (saltier than sweet soy) and the chili garlic (the spice counteracts the sweetness). Make sure your ratios are on point for this sauce, because it makes a difference.

Enrique Cruz, one of my longtime kitchen managers, searing off brisket before it hits the braising pan.

FOR THE DRY RUB

2 tablespoons vegetable oil

½ tablespoon kosher salt

¼ tablespoon freshly ground black pepper

½ teaspoon mustard powder

½ teaspoon chili powder

¼ tablespoon garlic powder

¼ tablespoon onion powder

1 tablespoon brown sugar

TO MAKE THE DRY RUB

Mix together all the dry rub ingredients in a small bowl.

FOR THE BRAISING LIQUID & BRISKET

3½ tablespoons vegetable oil

1 (4-pound) piece of brisket, first cut (the flat, leaner portion of the brisket) (see Note)

1 yellow onion, quartered

3 cloves garlic

3 bay leaves

1½ quarts beef broth

TO MAKE THE BRAISING LIQUID & BRISKET

1. Preheat the oven to 325°F.

2. Drizzle ½ tablespoon of the oil over the brisket and then spread the dry rub over the brisket.

3. Place a Dutch oven or a heavy-bottomed pot over medium-high heat and add 2 tablespoons of the oil to coat the pan. Sear the brisket on both sides for 3–4 minutes on each side until it has a nice sear (the meat will be browned, but make sure you don't char the outside). Remove the brisket and set it aside.

4. Reduce the heat to medium, add the remaining oil to coat the pan, then add the quartered onion and garlic cloves. Brown the onion and garlic cloves for 2–3 minutes, and then add the bay leaves. Turn off the heat.

5. Place the brisket back in the pot, with the fat cap facing up. Then add approximately 1 quart of the beef broth. The braising liquid should come halfway up the brisket. Depending on the size of the pot, you may need more or less braising liquid.

6. Cover the pan and braise the brisket at 325°F in the oven. After 2 hours, check the pan and see if additional beef broth needs to be added to ensure that the braising liquid is still halfway up the brisket.

7. Braise the brisket for an additional 2¼ hours. The brisket should be fork-tender when you take it out of the oven. Once the brisket is fork-tender, remove the brisket from the pot and strain the braising liquid. Discard the onions, garlic, and bay leaves. Using a large spoon, skim some of the liquid fat off the top of the strained braising liquid.

8. On a cutting board, chop the brisket while it is hot. If you are not serving the brisket immediately, pour a little of the braising liquid over the chopped brisket to keep it moist while it is refrigerated. Store the brisket in an airtight container in the fridge. The chopped brisket will keep for up to 3 days in the refrigerator.

. . . .

Note This recipe will yield around 2 ½ pounds of cooked brisket, more than the recipe for Southern Fun calls for. However, you can use the rest to make BBQ Brisket Tacos (page 74) or Brisket Grilled Cheese (page 81).

. . . .

FOR THE SOUTHERN FUN SAUCE

2¼ tablespoons light soy sauce

1 tablespoon Sweet Soy Sauce
  (see Asian Food Glossary, page 219)

2¼ tablespoons Oyster Sauce
  (see Asian Food Glossary, page 219)

3¼ tablespoons Chili Garlic Sauce
  (see Asian Food Glossary, page 219)

TO MAKE THE SOUTHERN FUN SAUCE

Whisk all the ingredients together.

ASSEMBLY

1 tablespoon vegetable oil

2 teaspoons garlic, minced (from 2 cloves, peeled)

2 teaspoons ginger, minced (from about ¼-inch knob, peeled)

¾ cup yellow onion, sliced

½ pound Braised Brisket, chopped
  (recipe above)

1½ pounds ho fun noodles (peeled) (see
  pages 12–13 for a description of how to
  prepare these noodles)

Pinch of white pepper

1½ cups kale, chiffonade (or thinly shredded)

1½ cups bean sprouts

¾ cup green onions, thinly sliced

¼ cup Fried Shallots (see Asian Food
  Glossary, page 219)

¼ cup cilantro, whole leaves, for garnish

1. Heat a wok or a wide nonstick stir-fry pan over medium-low heat and add the oil. Wait for the oil to shimmer, and then add the garlic and ginger. If the garlic starts to brown too quickly, reduce the heat.

2. Once the garlic and ginger are fragrant after about 30 seconds, add the onion and stir-fry it until it becomes translucent. This should take another 45 seconds to a minute. Add the brisket and stir-fry for an additional minute.

3. Add the ho fun noodles to the brisket mixture in the pan and stir them in over medium-high heat. Make sure to constantly turn the noodles when you stir-fry them so they don't stick to the bottom of the pan and burn. Don't be overly aggressive with the noodles, however, or they will break.

4. Once the noodles have cooked for 1 minute, add the Southern Fun sauce to the pan. Add a pinch of white pepper. Continue to stir-fry the noodles for another 2½–3 minutes.

5. Taste the noodles to make sure they are getting close to al dente. Add the kale and bean sprouts to the pan and stir-fry the noodles for another 30 seconds.

6. Take the noodles off the heat and plate them. Garnish the noodles with the green onions, fried shallots, and cilantro.

> **If your pan is not big enough, you may need to cook this dish in multiple rounds. That's fine. You can always cut your ingredients in half and repeat the process.**

MOM'S SHRIMP TOAST

Serves 5–10

My parents used to host a ton of dinner parties in our Tokyo condo. My mom almost always cooked for these parties. As people started to arrive and ring the doorbell, I remember my mom would split her time between saying hello to guests and firing up the first set of appetizers in the kitchen. One appetizer, which my mom always made for passing around, was shrimp toast. It's the consummate Chinese dish and a crowd-pleaser. Even though I'm allergic to shrimp, I would eat these toasts by the handful. I didn't care if I was going to break out in hives. It was worth it.

FOR THE TOAST

18 slices white sandwich bread, crusts cut off

¾ pound shrimp, peeled and deveined

¼ pound ground pork

3 tablespoons water chestnuts, roughly chopped

2 teaspoons garlic, minced

1½ teaspoons ginger, minced

½ egg, beaten

½ tablespoon sesame oil

½ tablespoon cornstarch

1½ tablespoons green onions, thinly chopped

¾ teaspoon salt

½ teaspoon white pepper

TO MAKE THE TOAST

1. Preheat the oven to 350°F.

2. Slice each piece of the sandwich bread into two rectangular slices and place them on two or three baking sheets.

3. Pulse the shrimp in a food processor. Do not overprocess the shrimp; it should feel like a rough chop and there should be texture to it.

4. Place the processed shrimp in a large mixing bowl and add all the remaining ingredients, except the sandwich bread, to the bowl. Mix all the ingredients together, then cover the bowl with plastic wrap and place it in the fridge.

5. Place the baking sheets in the oven, and toast the slices of sandwich bread until they are lightly browned and firm. This should take about 5 minutes.

6. Once the sandwich bread has cooled for 2–3 minutes, remove the shrimp mixture from the fridge and use a knife to smear it an even layer, about $1/4$- inch thick, on the top of each slice of bread. You do not want to make the layer too thick, or you will have to cook the toast longer and run the risk of discoloring the bread.

ASSEMBLY

2 quarts canola oil

1 cup Thai Chili Dipping Sauce (page 182)

Cilantro leaves, for garnish

Mint leaves, for garnish

Thai basil leaves, garnish

1. Heat the oil in a medium-size pot over medium-high heat until it reaches 350°F. Use a candy thermometer to gauge the temperature of the oil.

2. When the oil reaches 350°F, lay the shrimp toast facedown in the oil. It's important to lay the toast facedown initially, since you are cooking the shrimp paste, not the bread. Cook the shrimp paste, facedown, for 1 minute and 45 seconds. Flip the toast and cook the bottom of it for an additional 15 seconds (2 minutes total). A good rule of thumb is to look at the color of the bread to determine whether the toast is fully cooked. If the bread is golden brown, it's likely the shrimp paste has cooked through fully.

3. Place the fried toast on a roasting rack. Serve the toast with the Thai Chili Dipping Sauce and garnish the toast with cilantro, mint, and Thai basil.

SOY SAUCE CHICKEN

Serves 3–4

Soy sauce chicken, like chow fun, is one of those ultimate comfort foods for me. My mom always serves the chicken bone-in, and at room temperature, at our house. We nosh on the chicken with our hands and throw the bones onto a separate plate. It's okay to make this chicken a few hours ahead of time and let it sit at room temperature before eating. It's even good the next day . . . cold.

1 (3-pound) chicken (see Note)

6 (¼-inch) slices ginger, smashed

2 scallion stalks, cut into 3-inch pieces, smashed

½ teaspoon white pepper

1 tablespoon + ⅔ cup Dark Soy Sauce (see Asian Food Glossary, page 219)

1 tablespoon vegetable oil

5 cloves garlic, peeled and smashed

3 pods Star Anise (see Asian Food Glossary, page 219)

¾ cup Shaoxing Wine (see Asian Food Glossary, page 219)

¾ cup light soy sauce

⅓ cup sugar

1 teaspoon salt

1. Wash and dry the chicken. Rub the outside with 2 slices of the smashed ginger and 3–4 pieces of the smashed scallions. Coat the chicken with the white pepper and 1 tablespoon of dark soy sauce.

2. Use your hands to massage the dark soy sauce into the chicken. Place the chicken on a large plate and leave it uncovered in the refrigerator for 3–4 hours. Remove the chicken from the fridge about 1 hour before you are ready to cook it, so it will come up a little bit in temperature. This prevents the temperature of the poaching liquid from dropping too fast when you place the chicken in it.

3. Using a large, tall pot, heat the oil over medium-high heat. Then add the remaining ginger and the garlic. Brown the ginger and garlic for 3–4 minutes, and then add the remaining scallions and the star anise. While continuously stirring, cook the ingredients for 2 more minutes.

4. Add the Shaoxing wine and wait for it to start simmering, cooking off the alcohol. Add the light soy sauce, the remaining dark soy sauce, sugar, salt, and 8–10 cups water, depending on the size of the pot, and bring the entire mixture to a boil.

5. Lower the chicken gently into the mixture, using tongs. If you have tweezer tongs, use them (see Note). Since the chicken is not hot, it will lower the temperature of the liquid. Bring the liquid back to a boil over medium-high heat. Once it comes to a boil, reduce the heat immediately to an extremely low simmer. Simmer the chicken uncovered for 25 minutes.

6. After 25 minutes, turn off the heat and let the chicken sit in the pot, covered, for 10 more minutes. Take the temperature of the chicken in the thickest part of the breast using a meat thermometer to ensure that it is at least 165°F.

7. If the chicken is at temperature, remove the chicken and let it cool to room temperature. Break the chicken down, separating the thighs, breasts, wings, and drumsticks. At this point, you have two options. You can debone the breast and thighs, and then slice them. Alternatively, you can keep the bones in, and cut the chicken through the bone with a cleaver or a sharp knife.

8. Strain 1 cup of the soy sauce liquid into a separate saucepan and turn the heat on high. You can discard the remaining soy sauce liquid. Let the liquid boil for about 3–4 minutes until it is reduced by half. This will serve as a dipping sauce for the chicken, in addition to the ginger-scallion sauce. Soy sauce chicken is best accompanied by a nice steaming bowl of jasmine rice. Two cups of raw jasmine rice should be plenty for four people.

Note If you can spend a little extra money, I recommend getting a heritage-breed chicken. These chickens are typically smaller and cook more quickly than a standard 5-pound nonheritage variety. Because of the quicker cooking time, the meat, in turn, is a little juicier.

Note Use tweezer tongs, if you have them, to control the chicken (you can stick one end of the tongs into the cavity of the chicken) as you ease it into the liquid. Regular tongs will work fine, too. However, they have a tendency to offer less control and may tear the skin of the chicken once it has cooked.

CONGEE WITH SHIITAKE MUSHROOMS & BACON

Serves 4

Congee, rice porridge, or *jook*, as my mom referred to it, is another one of those cold-winter-night comfort foods I ate at home when I was growing up. My mom would fix a bowl of it for me if I had a cold or felt under the weather. While my mom's jook was served with shredded chicken and white pepper, this version amps it up a little with the use of dashi and some stronger-flavored toppings. If you don't have time to make your own chicken stock, you can always use store-bought chicken stock. The same is true of dashi—you can always use water as a substitute, if you don't have time to make it. For this recipe, I use a 10:1 ratio of water to rice, which is pretty standard. If you want a much thicker congee, you could go down to 8 cups of water to 1 cup of rice.

2 tablespoons vegetable oil

4 thinly sliced (about ⅛-inch-thick) medallions of ginger, skin on + 1 teaspoon minced ginger

4 cloves garlic (2 whole cloves, crushed; 2 cloves, minced)

2½ cups chicken stock (store-bought is fine)

2½ cups Dashi (page 167) or use 2½ cups water

½ cup rice, washed

¼ teaspoon white pepper + additional white pepper to taste

3–4 slices (about 5 ounces) thick-cut bacon, cut into ½-inch pieces

2 cups (about 3 ounces) shiitake mushrooms, stems removed, cleaned and sliced

½ tablespoon light soy sauce

¾ tablespoon Sweet Soy Sauce (see Asian Food Glossary, page 219)

Four 6-minute or 45-minute onsen eggs (page xv)

¼ cup green onions, chopped

¼ cup Fried Shallots (see Asian Food Glossary, page 219)

1. In a medium-size pot, heat 1 tablespoon of the oil over medium heat. Add the 4 slices of ginger and 2 whole cloves of garlic to the pot and sauté them until they are browned and aromatic (about 45 seconds to a minute).

2. Add the chicken stock, dashi, rice, and ¼ teaspoon of white pepper, and bring the mixture to a boil over high heat. It should take about 8–10 minutes for the liquid to reach a boil.

3. Once the mixture comes to a boil, reduce the heat to a simmer over low heat. Simmer the rice for 30 minutes. The rice will start to cook, swell up, and eventually break down. The liquid will look cloudy and white. At That point, take the rice off the heat. Once the rice has cooked and broken down, the congee will thicken quickly. You can add more chicken stock or dashi to loosen the congee as it sits.

4. In a separate pan, heat the remaining 1 tablespoon of oil over medium heat and add the bacon. Sauté the bacon until the fat is rendered (about 3–4 minutes), then add the shiitake mushrooms. If you want, you can discard the rendered fat into a heat-proof bowl before you add the mushrooms. Continue to sauté the bacon and mushrooms for an additional 2–3 minutes and then add the light soy sauce and the sweet soy sauce. Once the shiitakes have softened and cooked, after another 1–2 minutes, turn off the heat.

5. Ladle about 1 cup of the congee into each bowl and top it with the shiitakes and bacon. Place a 6-minute or 45-minute onsen egg on top of each bowl of congee. Garnish with green onions, fried shallots, and a pinch of white pepper.

KUNG PAO BRISKET

Serves 4

This recipe for kung pao comes closer than any other recipe in this book to a Chinese take-out dish. We have all had our moments with Chinese takeout and delivery. Maybe it was really cold outside and you just didn't want to go out. Maybe you were in college, didn't have a kitchen, and were craving cheap Chinese. Or maybe you were just drunk. Well, this dish may bring you back to those days, except the flavor profiles are a bit truer to the traditional spicy kung pao flavors, intertwined with peanuts, vegetables, and chilies. I recommend serving the Kung Pao Brisket with jasmine rice.

2 tablespoons soy sauce

2 teaspoons Shaoxing Wine (see Asian Food Glossary, page 219)

1 tablespoon Black Vinegar (see Asian Food Glossary, page 219)

1 tablespoon Tobanjan (see Asian Food Glossary, page 219)

1½ teaspoons sugar

1½ tablespoons + ¼ cup cornstarch

1¼ pounds Dry Rubbed Brisket (page 38), cut into cubes

2 quarts + 1 tablespoon vegetable oil

2 cloves garlic, minced

½ teaspoon ginger, grated

4 dried Thai Chilies (see Asian Food Glossary, page 219)

½ cup celery, diced

⅓ cup green onions, just the white part, chopped

½ cup leeks (white and light green parts only), sliced into ⅛-inch pieces

⅓ cup roasted peanuts, chopped in a food processor

¼ teaspoon toasted red Sichuan peppercorn powder (see Note)

¼ cup green onions, chopped

4 cups jasmine rice, cooked

. . . .

Note To make your own Sichuan peppercorn powder, take a handful of red Sichuan peppercorns and place them in a dry skillet. Toast them over medium-low heat. They will start to become fragrant after 5–6 minutes. At this point, remove the peppercorns from the heat and grind them in a spice grinder. The ground Sichuan peppercorns can be stored in an airtight container for up to 3–4 months.

. . . .

1. Mix the soy sauce, Shaoxing wine, black vinegar, tobanjan, and sugar together in a small bowl and set it aside. This is your kung pao sauce.

2. In a separate, small bowl, mix 1½ tablespoons of cornstarch with 2 tablespoons of water to make a slurry. The slurry will help thicken your sauce.

3. In a mixing bowl, dredge the brisket in the remaining ¼ cup of cornstarch. Using a fine- mesh strainer, shake off any extra cornstarch and set the brisket aside.

4. Heat the 2 quarts of oil in a Dutch oven or a large cast iron skillet until the oil reaches 350°F. When the oil has come to temperature, add the coated brisket to the hot oil and deep-fry it for 45 seconds to 1 minute. You are just trying to crisp the brisket and let it turn golden brown.

5. In a wok or a large pan on low heat, heat the remaining 1 tablespoon of oil. When the oil starts to shimmer, add the garlic, ginger, and Thai chiles and sauté them for 45 seconds until they become aromatic.

6. Increase the heat to medium-high and add the celery to the pan. Stir-fry the celery for 2 minutes, and then add the green-onion whites and the leeks. Continue to stir-fry all the ingredients together for an additional minute.

7. Add the fried brisket, roasted peanuts, kung pao sauce, and cornstarch slurry, and continue to stir-fry for an additional minute.

8. Remove the kung pao brisket from the pan and top it with the Sichuan peppercorn powder and green onions.

9. Serve the kung pao brisket with a steaming bowl of jasmine rice.

SCRAMBLED EGGS WITH CHINESE CHIVES

Serves 3-4

I'm not sure whether you would classify this dish as Japanese or Chinese, but it was a dish I grew up eating at home. It's pretty quick and easy to put together, and it is great served with a bowl of rice for breakfast, lunch, or dinner. The addition of a little water and sugar with the eggs helps to give them a fluffier texture. Also, be liberal with the amount of oil you use in your wok or pan. It will help keep the eggs from sticking to the pan.

5 eggs

¼ teaspoon white pepper

¼ teaspoon sesame oil

¼ teaspoon sugar

½ teaspoon soy sauce

1 teaspoon Shaoxing Wine (see Asian Food Glossary, page 219)

¼ teaspoon salt

3 tablespoons vegetable oil

2 cloves peeled garlic, minced

1½ cups Chinese chives or garlic chives (cut into ½-inch pieces)

2 tablespoons Chili Garlic Sauce (see Asian Food Glossary, page 219)

1. Crack the eggs into a medium-size bowl and add the white pepper, sesame oil, sugar, soy sauce, Shaoxing wine, 1 tablespoon of water, and salt. Beat the mixture together with a fork until all the seasonings have been incorporated into the beaten eggs.

2. Heat the oil in a wok or a large skillet over low heat. Once the oil starts to shimmer, add the garlic. Stir-fry the garlic for about 45 seconds until it is aromatic.

3. Add the Chinese chives to the pan. Stir-fry the chives for 2 minutes, or until they have started to wilt.

4. Add the eggs to the pan. Once a thin, cooked layer of eggs forms on the bottom of the pan, stir the eggs. Continue to do so, as the bottom of the egg mixture cooks. It's important to continue to move the eggs in the pan or they will burn. Pick up the pan and move the egg mixture around so that the raw beaten eggs cover the remainder of the pan.

5. Continue to cook the scrambled eggs to the desired level of doneness. I prefer my eggs on the drier side, so I like to cook them a little bit longer for about 1½–2 minutes total.

6. Serve the eggs with a side of chili garlic sauce.

CHINESE BROCCOLI WITH YUZU & BONITO

Serves 4

When my mom cooked Chinese food at home, one of her go-to side dishes was always Chinese broccoli with oyster sauce and white pepper. The broccoli was steamed first, and then pan-fried to give it some texture. This is an updated version of that dish.

1 pound Chinese broccoli, trimmed and stalks split (see Note)

3 tablespoons vegetable oil

¼ teaspoon kosher salt

¼ teaspoon white pepper

½ teaspoon Shiitake Powder (see To Make the Tofu, #3, page 149)

1 tablespoon Yuzu Juice (see Asian Food Glossary, page 219)

½ cup Bonito Flakes (see Asian Food Glossary, page 219)

Note Chinese broccoli has really thick stalks that can be difficult to cook all the way through, compared to the leafy greens at the top, which do not take long to cook. This is why I recommend trimming and discarding about ¼ inch off the bottom of the Chinese broccoli stalks and splitting the larger stalks in half lengthwise down the middle. You will need to cut around the leaves at the top, where they meet the stem, in order to keep them intact. Splitting the stalks will allow for a quicker cooking time and a better result overall.

1. Coat the Chinese broccoli with 2 tablespoons of the oil, then season it aggressively with the kosher salt and white pepper.

2. Heat the remaining 1 tablespoon of oil in a wide skillet or pan, over medium-high heat. Once the pan is hot, add the Chinese broccoli. Make sure not to crowd the pan. You may need to cook the broccoli in two rounds.

3. After you've added the broccoli to the pan, add 1/2 cup of water, in order to steam the broccoli. Cover the pan with a lid.

4. Once the broccoli has steamed for 1 minute, remove the lid and increase the heat to high. Let the broccoli continue to cook in the pan. Once the water has evaporated, you can get a hard char on the broccoli by weighing it down in the pan while it cooks over high heat. I like to place a small cast iron skillet right on top of the broccoli. This presses on the broccoli, spreads it out, and exposes the greatest amount of surface area of the broccoli to hit the pan.

5. After another 1 1/2 minutes of cooking, remove the broccoli. The broccoli should be charred, particularly the upper leaf areas. Top the broccoli with the shiitake powder, yuzu juice, and bonito flakes.

JAPANESE-AMERICAN FAST FOOD

Opposite: Kentucky Fried Chicken™ in Tokyo, Japan. My dad worked for the company when I was growing up in Japan.

My Japanese "grandparents" took my dad into their home when he was a college student studying abroad.

often joke that I have a Chinese mother and a Japanese father. It's a joke because my dad, Joel, is a white Jewish guy from Mt. Vernon, New York. But really, my dad should probably be recognized as an honorary Japanese. He's fluent in the language and has written a book about Japanese businessmen *in Japanese.* He even pushes his way through the Japanese train stations like a real Japanese.

I've always respected my dad and what he's been able to accomplish in life. He studied abroad in Japan when he was in college and lived with a Japanese family. My dad's parents both had passed by the time he finished college, forcing him to fend for himself at an early age. He assimilated in Japan quickly, learning the language, adopting Japanese customs, and embracing the Japanese way (for the most part). I remember him telling me that he once asked his host "mother" if she would buy some orange juice for him. After she bought it, he found out that a pint of orange juice cost $8, and that he was asking for a luxury purchase. He was embarrassed that he had asked his host mother to spring for such a pricey drink, but he could only learn Japanese culture through trial and error.

Although my dad lived in Hong Kong and Singapore after he graduated from college, he eventually landed in Japan once again in the early 1980s, when I was born. My dad took a job with Kentucky Fried Chicken™. Yes, *that* Kentucky Fried Chicken. What's unique about American fast food in Japan, however, is that it is nothing like American fast food. The food quality is significantly better (the Japanese have high standards), the stores are immaculate, and the service is impeccable. Restaurant staff members are always properly uniformed and work together like a well-oiled machine. I remember going to watch basketball games at my

Kentucky Fried Chicken had a farm in Japan. I'm not making this up. With real chickens that laid real eggs.

high school on the weekends and always making a pit stop at the local KFC first. There is nothing quite like plunging your hand into a paper bag filled with hot, buttery biscuits and *Japanese* Kentucky Fried Chicken.

When I wasn't feasting on KFC, my parents would take me and my sister to MOS Burger®, the epitome of Japanese-American fusion, where the mad Japanese food scientists mixed teriyaki sauce with burgers and put miso beef ragu on hamburger patties. I loved MOS Burger. It had such an impact on me that I would later open a Japanese-inspired burger truck called Yume Burger in 2012. Unfortunately, Yume Burger was short-lived, as the concept never truly took off. There was too much of a learning curve for people to really grasp exactly what a Japanese-inspired burger is.

My dad's job with KFC really opened my eyes to the restaurant business at an early age. It was the initial gateway that showed me everything behind the scenes. My dad took me to different units and would talk to store managers. He would assess food quality and any operational issues plaguing each store. We would always discuss the strengths and weaknesses of each store after visiting them. At a young age, I was already getting an earful about restaurant operations and traits to look for in the successful ones.

After a few years with KFC, my dad broke the big news as my family sat down for dinner at the Tokyo American Club one evening. He had taken a job within the PepsiCo™ family, with Pizza Hut®. My parents felt that it was time for my sister and me to live in the United States. We had spent our entire childhoods in Japan and only knew American culture through Japanese MTV, Steven Seagal ads, and the yearly summer vacation to visit my cousins in Huntington Beach, California. My sister and I naturally asked, "Where in the States?" My dad responded, "Atlanta." I remember realizing, at that exact moment, the magnitude of the challenge I was about to face as an eleven-year-old. Not only did I have to learn American culture, but I had to learn American culture in the South, a region of the United States I knew next to nothing about. It was a move I tepidly embraced.

Above: The MOS Burger menu that inspired me to start Yume Burger.
Opposite: The MOS Burger teriyaki burger—the ultimate Japanese-American mash-up.

JAPAJAM BURGER

Serves 4

The JapaJam burger was our attempt, at Yume Burger, to re-create the umami-level explosiveness of MOS Burger. Ours really stopped and started with the tomato jam. We tried to re-create the "miso tomato meat sauce" that MOS Burger uses on one of their most popular burgers. Tomatoes have a certain level of umami that can really elevate a dish. We paired the tomato jam with a hoisin-based sauce that was somewhat like our version of teriyaki sauce. To this day, I'm still surprised that the JapaJam burger didn't single-handedly keep the Yume Burger truck afloat. It lives on, however, in our restaurant.

FOR THE TEMPURA-BATTERED ONION STRINGS

Makes about 2 cups

2 quarts vegetable oil

1 yellow onion, sliced very thinly, widthwise, on a mandoline

12 ounces Shiner Bock® or another American-style dark lager

1 cup dry Tempura mix (page 227)

TO MAKE THE TEMPURA-BATTERED ONION STRINGS

1. Pour the oil into a large, deep saucepan or pot, and heat the oil until it reaches 350°F (see page xv for directions on frying).

2. Soak the sliced onion in the lager, and then remove it. Dredge the wet onion in the tempura batter. Gently shake the onion in a fine mesh strainer or colander to release any excess batter. When the oil reaches 350°F, place the onion in the hot oil and fry it for 20 seconds, or until it is lightly browned. Remove the onion strings from the oil and place them on top of a paper towel–lined plate.

FOR THE BURGER PATTIES

1¼ pounds ground beef, chuck (80/20)

Salt and pepper to taste

TO MAKE THE BURGER PATTIES

Form the ground beef into four 5-ounce patties, and season them with salt and pepper. The patties should be relatively wide (about 5 inches) and only about ¼-inch thick.

ASSEMBLY

1 tablespoon butter

4 hamburger buns (preferably potato or challah)

2 tablespoons vegetable oil

4 eggs

Salt and pepper to taste

½ cup Tomato Jam (page 184)

4 slices jalapeño jack cheese

½ cup Chinese BBQ Sauce (page 167)

1. Heat a wide pan over medium-low heat. Place the butter in the pan. When the butter melts, add the buns to the pan, facedown. Flip the buns when the face sides are browned (but not burned).

2. While the buns are toasting, add 1 tablespoon of the oil to a separate steel skillet or cast iron pan, set over medium high heat. Begin cooking the burgers. To cook a medium burger, flip the patty when you start to see the blood rise to the top of the burger.

3. After you have flipped the burgers, add the remaining 1 tablespoon of oil to a third pan—this one nonstick—over medium-low heat. Once the oil starts to shimmer, drop the eggs into the nonstick pan and season them with salt and pepper. Fry the eggs sunny side up for 2–3 minutes and remove them from the heat when they are done. The yolks should not be overcooked and should break when pierced. If you are worried about the timing of the fried eggs, you can always cook them beforehand and keep them warm on the stovetop.

4. As the burgers and eggs finish cooking, remove the buns from the heat and spoon some of the tomato jam onto the bottom bun.

5. About 1¹/₂ minutes after the burgers have been flipped, place the slices of jalapeño jack on top of the burgers. Add a couple of tablespoons of water in the pan and cover. Let the cheese melt on the burger for an additional 45 seconds.

6. Once the cheese has melted, place the burger on the bottom half of the bun with the tomato jam. Top the burger with a fried egg. Then, gently place the tempura fried onion strings on top.

7. Spoon the Chinese BBQ sauce on top of the onion strings, and then place the top of the bun on the burger.

I really like to cook my burgers in a cast iron skillet. The cast iron gets very hot and allows you to develop a crust on the outside of the burger. I recommend having at least two or three different sizes of cast iron skillets in your kitchen to accommodate whatever you happen to be cooking.

YUME DOG

Serves 4

Growing up in Japan, I was infatuated with Japanese burgers. Fusion, in my opinion, gets a bad rap because it's not traditional. But who gives a shit if it's not traditional as long as it tastes good? The Japanese fuse everything, including their fast food. As a kid, I craved the teriyaki burger at McDonald's, and eventually graduated to MOS Burger, the mecca of Japanese-inspired burgers. In my opinion, there is no better fast-food joint *in the world* than MOS Burger. The movement to fuse Japanese flavors with American staples continued stateside, after Japadog was launched in Canada, and copycats started to open up shop in Seattle. Creating a Japanese-inspired hot dog was by no means my idea. But this dog is unique to the Yume Burger concept I created. I wanted to fuse the very American flavor of a hot dog with the Japanese flavors of tonkatsu sauce, wasabi, and nori.

The legendary tonkatsu house, Tonki, in Tokyo, Japan. There are only two items served: fatty pork tonkatsu and lean pork tonkatsu. Both are served with shredded cabbage, hot mustard, rice, and, of course, tonkatsu sauce.

4 hot dog buns

½ tablespoon vegetable oil

4 jumbo Hebrew National® kosher all beef franks

2 cups, Tempura-Battered Onion Strings (page 59)

4 tablespoons Wasabi Mayo (page 186)

4 tablespoons Tonkatsu Sauce (page 185)

¼ cup shredded Nori (see Asian Food Glossary, page 219)

1. Using a serrated knife, slice the buns from the top as opposed to the side. You will be laying the hot dog into the bun from the top, as you would lay lobster into a Connecticut lobster roll.

2. In a medium-size skillet, heat the oil over medium heat and lay the hot dogs in the pan. Turn the hot dogs so that they cook on all sides. This should take about 4 minutes. Remove the hot dogs from the heat and transfer them to a separate plate.

3. In the same pan in which you cooked the hot dogs, lay the buns, split side down, until they brown a little. Once they have browned, flip the buns to toast the other sides.

4. Remove the buns from the pan and stuff the hot dogs into the buns.

5. Lay the tempura-battered onion strings on top of the hot dogs. Then top the hot dogs with the wasabi mayo, tonkatsu sauce, and shredded nori.

We use a local bakery at Peached. One thing to note when you purchase buns: I personally like a good hot dog–to–bun ratio. Buns that are too big can overpower the hot dog. The bigger the bun, the bigger the hot dog you should try to source. If you do end up buying a larger bun, you can always cut off the sides a little bit, just as you might trim a bun for a lobster roll. I suggest a lightweight bun that won't overpower this hot dog.

SOCIAL BURGER

Serves 4

Where the JapaJam burger was our riff on the original burger from MOS Burger (miso red sauce, tomatoes), the Social Burger is our version of the Asian Big Mac™, only with better ingredients. We needed a dish at the restaurant that would get people into the door for Happy Hour. From our point of view, the Social Burger is slightly more approachable than the JapaJam. It has familiar ingredients, like pickles, American cheese, and a "special sauce." If McDonald's hired an Asian chef on steroids, this burger would likely be the result. The Peached Sauce, Miso Caramelized Onions, and Japanese Sesame Pickles can all be made 1–2 days ahead of time.

FOR THE BURGER PATTIES

1¼ pounds chuck beef (80/20)

Kosher salt to taste

Freshly ground black pepper to taste

TO MAKE THE BURGER PATTIES

Shape the ground meat into four 5-ounce patties and season them with the salt and pepper. The patties should be relatively wide (about 5 inches) and only about ¼-inch thick.

FOR THE PEACHED SAUCE

Makes a little less than ½ cup

¼ cup mayonnaise

¾ teaspoon horseradish, prepared

1 tablespoon Mae Ploy (sweet chili sauce) (see Asian Food Glossary, page 219) or substitute with 1 tablespoon Thai Chili Dipping Sauce (page 182)

¾ teaspoon Worcestershire sauce

¾ tablespoon Kimchi (page 173), pureed (see Note below)

TO MAKE THE PEACHED SAUCE

Whisk all the ingredients together in a small mixing bowl. You can always make this sauce ahead of time and refrigerate it.

. . . .

Note You can always use store-bought kimchi for this recipe, if you don't have time to make your own.

. . . .

FOR THE MISO CARAMELIZED ONIONS

Makes about 1 cup (see Note)

2 tablespoons vegetable oil

1 large yellow onion, julienned

1¼ tablespoon Shiro (white) Miso (see Asian Food Glossary, page 219)

½ tablespoon brown sugar

½ cup Sake (see Asian Food Glossary, page 219)

TO MAKE THE MISO CARAMELIZED ONIONS

1. In a wide-bottomed skillet or pot with a large surface area, heat the oil over medium heat. Sauté the onion slices with the miso and brown sugar until they are browned. This should take 10–15 minutes.

2. Add ¼ cup of the sake to the pan and continue to stir the onions for 20 minutes over medium-low heat until the onions really start to caramelize. You will want to keep an eye on the onions and stir them constantly. Otherwise, they will burn in the pan. The onions should turn a dark shade of brown.

3. Deglaze the pan with the remaining sake and stir the onions for an additional 5 minutes. Take the onions off the heat.

4. Store the onions for up to 5 days in an airtight container, refrigerated.

. . . .

Note This recipe yields more onions than you need for the burgers, but you can always store the onions and add them to a sandwich or eat them with eggs for breakfast.

. . . .

ASSEMBLY

1 tablespoon butter

4 sturdy hamburger buns (preferably potato or challah)

2 tablespoons vegetable oil

4 tablespoons Peached Sauce (recipe above)

1 cup iceberg lettuce, finely shredded

4 slices American cheese

¼ cup Miso Caramelized Onions (recipe above)

12 slices Japanese Sesame Pickles (page 171)

1. Heat a large pan over medium-low heat, and then place the butter in the pan until it melts. Add the buns facedown. Flip the buns when the face sides are browned (but not burned).

2. In a separate cast iron or steel skillet, heat the oil over medium heat. Once the oil starts to shimmer, begin cooking the burgers. You want to get a hard sear on your burger, so look for a crust when you flip it. To cook a medium burger, flip it as soon you start to see the blood rise to the top of the patty. Continue to cook the burger for another 2 minutes after you've flipped it.

3. As your burgers finish cooking, remove the buns from the heat and spoon some of the Peached Sauce onto the bottom halves of the buns. Add ¼ cup of the iceberg lettuce on top of the sauce.

4. Once the burgers are about 45 seconds away from the desired doneness, add a slice of American cheese on top of each burger, add 2 tablespoons of water into the pan and cover the pan to help the cheese melt.

5. When the cheese has melted, remove the burgers from the pan and place them on top of the bottom halves of the buns. Top the burgers with miso caramelized onions. Then, gently lay three Japanese sesame pickles on top of each burger and cover it with the top of the bun.

Since this recipe calls for hamburger patties with a high fat content, and there are a lot of toppings on the burger, I really recommend a sturdy bun that can withstand a bit of wetness from dripping fat. The more substantial the bun, the better.

TEMPURA FISH BURGER

Serves 4

This recipe is another dish from the now-defunct Yume Burger food truck. What makes it special is the flaky crust of the tempura-battered catfish, combined with the crispy cool crunch of the slaw and the subtle, but sophisticated flavor profile of the Japanese tartar sauce. My parents used to take me to dinner at old-school tempura restaurants in Japan, where you could have a multicourse tempura dinner for $50 a head. There was almost always a tempura whitefish course. My goal is to evoke this experience in a sandwich.

FOR THE TEMPURA BATTER

1 cup Tempura Flour (see Asian Food Glossary, page 219)

6 ounces very cold, nonflavored sparkling water

TO MAKE THE TEMPURA BATTER

Whisk together the tempura flour and sparkling water in a large mixing bowl. The batter should be relatively thick and coat the back of a spoon. If it is too thick, add more sparkling water to the batter. If it is too thin, add more tempura flour.

One of the tricks to making a good tempura batter is to use very cold sparkling water. Place a chilled can of sparkling water in the freezer for 15 minutes before you add it to the batter.

FOR THE ASIAN SLAW

1 cup purple cabbage, shredded thinly
  on a mandoline

⅓ cup green cabbage, shredded thinly
  on a mandoline

½ cup carrots, peeled and julienned

3 tablespoons green onions, sliced on a bias
  ¼ inch wide

3 tablespoons cilantro, whole pieces

3½ tablespoons Wasabi Mayo (page 186)

Kosher salt to taste

Freshly ground black pepper to taste

TO MAKE THE ASIAN SLAW

Combine the purple cabbage, green cabbage, carrots, green onions, cilantro, and wasabi mayo in a mixing bowl. Season the slaw with a pinch of salt and black pepper to taste.

To properly shred cabbage on a mandoline, you do not need a blade insert—the mandoline has a flat blade built in. Start by removing the outer layer of the cabbage. Split the cabbage in half with a knife, and then cut the cabbage in half again, making sure to slice through the core of the cabbage. You should have four pieces at this point. Remove the core from each piece of cabbage. Hold the cabbage lengthwise and move it back and forth over the blade in the mandolin. If the shreds of cabbage are too thick, tighten the settings underneath the mandoline in order to shorten the gap between the blade and the body of the mandoline. Protect your fingers, throughout the process, by moving at a slow pace and laying the cabbage against the palm of your hand, with your fingers parallel to your palm. This will prevent your fingers from being exposed to the blade.

ASSEMBLY

2 quarts vegetable oil

4 (4-ounce) catfish fillets

4 hamburger buns (preferably potato or challah)

1 tablespoon butter

4 tablespoons Japanese Tartar Sauce
  (page 172)

16 Japanese Sesame Pickles (page 171)

1. Pour the oil into a large, deep frying pan and heat the oil until it reaches 350°F.

2. When the oil is at temperature, slowly dip the catfish fillets into the tempura batter. The batter should coat the catfish nicely and not immediately run off. If the batter runs off, it is too thin. However, if the batter does not move at all on the fish, it is too thick.

3. Gently place the batter-coated fillets in the pan and fry them over high heat for 2½–3 minutes. Make sure to keep an eye on the temperature of your oil once you start frying the fish. If you notice the temperature starting to drop, you can increase the heat on your burner. After the fish is cooked, remove the fillets from the oil and place them on a cooling rack with a rimmed baking sheet underneath it (or you can place the fillets on a plate lined with paper towels).

4. Place the butter in a separate, wide skillet and let it melt over medium-low heat. When the butter has melted, add the buns facedown. Flip the buns when the face side is browned (but not burned).

5. Spoon a tablespoon of Japanese tartar sauce on the bottom of each bun, then top the tartar sauce with a fillet. Place a heaping spoonful of Asian slaw on top of the catfish fillet, followed by four Japanese sesame pickles. Cover the pickles with the top bun.

UMAMI FRIED CHICKEN

Serves 4

We do a Fried Chicken and Whiskey Night at the restaurant that epitomizes the best of Southern and Asian cooking. Our fried chicken is marinated overnight in a blend of Asian ingredients and instead of dredging the chicken in buttermilk and flour, we use rice flour for a crisper crunch. While this chicken recipe isn't meant to be Japanese KFC, I think it makes a damn good case for Thai KFC. You can serve the chicken with a side of Dashi Bacon Braised Kale (page 78) or Wasabi Mashed Potatoes (page 90). Scrap the turkey for Thanksgiving and run with this meal.

FOR THE MARINATED CHICKEN

1 cup Fish Sauce (see Asian Food Glossary, page 219)

¼ cup Rice Wine Vinegar (see Asian Food Glossary, page 219)

½ cup sugar

1 cup water

2 tablespoons lime juice

2 tablespoons Chili Garlic Sauce (see Asian Food Glossary, page 219)

6 cloves garlic

1 (3½–4 pound) chicken, broken down into 2 legs, 2 thighs, 2 whole wings, and 4 pieces of breast (breast is split) (see Note)

TO MAKE THE MARINATED CHICKEN

1. Puree all of the ingredients, except for the chicken, in a blender.

2. Marinate the broken-down chicken in the fish sauce marinade overnight in a large airtight container or resealable bag.

Note I recommend asking your butcher to break the chicken down for you into these quantities. Alternatively, you can purchase drumsticks, thighs, and wings separately.

FOR THE BATTER

1½ cups rice flour

TO MAKE THE BATTER

Whisk the rice flour and 1½ cups of cold water in a mixing bowl and set the batter aside. The consistency of the mixture should be thick enough to heavily coat the back of a spoon.

As the batter sits, the rice flour will slowly separate from the water. So make sure to whisk the batter right before you dip the chicken into it.

ASSEMBLY

2 quarts vegetable oil

1. Place the pieces of chicken on a baking sheet. Set the oven to 350°F and bake the chicken for 30 minutes. (You are parbaking the chicken, since it is difficult to control the temperature of a deep fryer at home.) Using a meat thermometer, check the temperature of the chicken while it is in the oven to make sure it reaches 165°F. It's best to take the temperature of the thickest part of the breast, since this is the thickest cut of meat you are cooking off. When the chicken is at temperature, remove it from the oven and set it in the refrigerator to cool. You can remove the chicken from the refrigerator when it is cold to the touch.

2. Once the chicken has cooled in the refrigerator, heat 2 quarts of oil to 350°F in a medium-size pot.

3. When the oil is at 350°F, coat the parbaked chicken in the rice flour batter and then place the chicken in the hot oil. The rice flour batter should be thick enough so it does not run off the chicken. If the rice flour batter has been sitting for a few minutes, make sure to give it a stir right before you dip the chicken in the batter.

4. Let the chicken cook in the oil for 2–3 minutes. It should turn a robust brown. Do not let the chicken get too brown or dark.

5. Remove the chicken from the oil and place it on a cooling rack with a rimmed baking sheet underneath it for 2 minutes before serving.

4

SOUTHERN COMFORT
& THE PEACH STATE

Opposite: The pass at the restaurant. The last checkpoint before food is run to the tables.

They say that change is a good thing. It sure didn't feel that way to me. Upon arriving in the United States in 1995, at the age of eleven, I felt the impact of cultural change almost immediately. My parents made the decision to send me to private school, where I was going to be the only Asian kid in my entire class of nearly one hundred kids. Even though I was an American, I didn't feel culturally American. Instead, I went from feeling accepted in a culturally diverse environment in Tokyo to feeling nervous about my new, extremely nondiverse environment. As a result of my unorthodox upbringing, fitting into the Southern milieu was a challenge from the start. I was a half-Chinese, half–non-practicing Jewish kid who grew up in Tokyo, Japan with a bunch of international kids. I had adopted an international culture, but certainly not an American one. And now for the first time I was being thrust into a predominantly white private school that was infused with fifty-plus years of Southern culture. As much as I love my parents, they did not prepare me for the cultural transition I was about to make. I was left to figure it out for myself.

I had to process American culture—how to eat, talk, dress, and socialize. Early on, I was completely lost. On my first day of school in seventh grade, my mom packed some snacks in a Japanese-style plastic bento box for me to eat between periods. The lid of the box was secured with a Hello Kitty® elastic band. Inside were all sorts of snacks, like onigiri and Pocky® sticks. It didn't take long for the other students to ask probing, judgmental questions. "What are you eating?" "What's that smell?" "Y'all eat that?" To them the food was as much of a cultural surprise as their reaction was to me. I remember thinking, "What's wrong with what I'm eating?" "Why the fuck would I want to eat cafeteria nachos?"

My lack of American style also shocked my classmates. As an eleven-year-old, I had no idea how Americans attending a private school were supposed to dress. All of a sudden, boots, flannel, and long-sleeved tees were the norm. I was wearing the bright-green sweatshirt from The GAP® that my mom had bought for me. I think it's fair to say that I got a lot of grief for that bright-green sweatshirt. I was teased and picked on for being different. Here I was, a kid transplanted to Atlanta from Tokyo. I dressed differently, talked differently, and even ate differently. I had zero knowledge of Southern American private school culture. I was an easy target.

When I look back on that time, I still get stressed. It wasn't an easy transition by any measure. There is no book that teaches an eleven-year-old how to adapt to a new culture. But I also think the experiences I had strengthened me. They hardened me. They led me to believe that I could tackle other tough periods in my life, if I could survive them. I firmly believe that I am the product of my experiences. The challenges I faced early on helped prepare me to take on new challenges. Little did I know, at the age of eleven, that I was already developing the skills I'd need to succeed in the food-truck and restaurant world.

BBQ BRISKET TACOS

Serves 4

This is one of the original tacos from the food truck that we serve at the restaurant. It was one of my first menu creations, before I even left my law gig. In the South, and especially in Texas, *brisket* is a trigger that summons a deep sense of comfort. People's eyes just naturally light up when they see it on a menu. This BBQ brisket taco is really well received at the restaurant because it isn't overpowering and appeals to anyone who is already familiar with brisket.

FOR THE CREAMY APPLE SLAW

4 cups green cabbage, thinly sliced on a mandoline

1½ cups carrots, peeled and julienned

½ green apple, julienned

1 teaspoon sugar

2 tablespoons mayonnaise

1 teaspoon Rice Wine Vinegar (see Asian Food Glossary, page 219)

Kosher salt to taste

Freshly ground black pepper to taste

TO MAKE THE CREAMY APPLE SLAW

Mix all the ingredients together in mixing bowl.

ASSEMBLY

8 (5-inch) tortillas (flour or corn)

1 pound Dry Rubbed Brisket, braised and chopped (page 38)

½ cup Peach BBQ Sauce (page 177)

1. Place a large dry skillet over medium heat, and then heat the tortillas on both sides for 20 seconds per side.

2. Place about 2 ounces of brisket on top of each tortilla, then add 2 tablespoons of creamy apple slaw and a tablespoon of peach BBQ sauce on top.

SHRIMP, BACON & GOUDA GRITS

Serves 4

Whenever I think of grits, I always think of the movie *My Cousin Vinny*, where Joe Pesci plays a New York "lawyer," and has to try a murder case in Alabama. He stops in a diner and asks the cook what a grit is. If you grow up in the South, you have to know what a grit is. All self-respecting Southerners love to eat grits, whether it's at home or at Waffle House. So here's my homage to grits, and, no, these aren't instant.

FOR THE GRITS

4 cups Dashi (page 167)

¾ teaspoon kosher salt

2 tablespoons unsalted butter

1 cup stone-ground white grits

1 cup whole milk

¼ teaspoon freshly ground black pepper

4 ounces smoked Gouda, grated in
   medium-size-hole box grater

TO MAKE THE GRITS

1. Bring the dashi, salt, and 1 tablespoon of the butter to a boil in a medium-size pan. Once the dashi starts to boil, slowly add the grits and whisk them in. Constantly whisk the grits into the dashi. You will see some of the corn hulls (chaff) rise to the top. The chaff can make the grits texturally unpleasant and take away from their overall creaminess, so I recommend skimming the chaff off the top of the liquid.

2. Reduce the heat to a simmer and continue to whisk the grits. The first 10–15 minutes of whisking are very important, as you want the water to get absorbed into the grits and the grits to thicken.

3. Stir in $1/2$ cup of the milk and continue to simmer the grits in the pan, partially covered, for 10 minutes, whisking every few minutes, so that the grits do not stick to the bottom of the pan. Pour in the remaining $1/2$ cup of milk, and continue to simmer the grits in the pan, partially covered, for another 30 minutes. Continue to whisk the grits, every so often, while they are simmering. The grits should be creamy at this point. (They will still have some texture toward the back of your tongue, but overall the grits should be smooth.)

4. Turn off the heat and incorporate the remaining 1 tablespoon of butter, the black pepper, and the smoked Gouda into the grits.

If you don't serve grits right away, they will thicken quickly, even if you have them on low heat. I would recommend keeping a little extra dashi or milk on hand to whisk into the grits, so that you can thin them out to your taste. If you have any left over, you can always store and reheat them the next day. You'll just need to rehydrate the grits with a little more dashi, milk, or water.

If you don't have dashi on hand, you can always use unsalted chicken broth as a substitute, or even water. I personally feel dashi really enhances the flavor of the grits and is worth going the extra mile.

FOR THE SHRIMP & BACON

¾ pound (12–14) medium-size shrimp, peeled and deveined

Pinch of kosher salt

Pinch of freshly ground black pepper

6 ounces thick-sliced bacon, cut into about 5 (⅛-inch) pieces

1 tablespoon vegetable oil

TO MAKE THE SHRIMP & BACON

1. Season the shrimp with kosher salt and black pepper.

2. Place a medium-size cast iron pan or steel skillet over medium heat. Place the bacon in the pan. The goal is to give the bacon some crispiness, so you want it to brown a little bit. This should take no longer than 4–5 minutes. Once the bacon is cooked, remove it from the pan and place it on a paper towel–lined plate.

3. With the pan still on medium heat, add the oil. Once the oil starts to shimmer, add the shrimp to the pan. Cook the shrimp for about 2 minutes on one side, until browned. Turn the shrimp over and cook them for another 2 minutes.

4. Touch the shrimp to see if they have finished cooking. The shrimp should be semi-firm when you touch them with your index finger. Turn the heat off and place the shrimp on a plate, so they stop cooking.

ASSEMBLY

4 eggs, cooked 6 minutes in boiling-hot water or onsen tamagos (see Cooking Notes, page xv)

2 ounces Gouda cheese, grated

2 full stems of green onion (green portions and white, if desired) or chives, thinly sliced

1. In a small saucepot, boil 2 quarts of water. Add the eggs and boil them for 6 minutes. When they're done, immediately shock them in ice water. Peel the eggs after they have been shocked and set them aside.

2. Spoon a portion of the grits into a bowl.

3. Top the grits with an egg, 3 whole shrimp, and a little bit of bacon.

4. Garnish the bowl with some additional grated Gouda and sliced green onions.

As an alternative to boiling the egg, you can use an immersion circulator to cook it sous vide (see Cooking Notes, page xvi). The result is an egg with a softer white (onsen tamago, see photo on page 45).

DASHI BACON BRAISED KALE

In high school, our soccer team used to take weekend road trips to the countryside in Georgia. My favorite part of these trips was eating at Southern restaurants for lunch, after the game, and feasting on fried chicken, biscuits, mashed potatoes, gravy, and collard greens. While braised kale is used in this recipe, rather than collards, the flavor comes close. The smokiness of the bacon pairs beautifully with the Dashi, and the sweetness of the Mirin helps balance out some of the bitter notes of the kale. I recommend pairing this dish with Umami Fried Chicken (page 68.)

2 tablespoons vegetable oil

3 slices thick cut bacon, roughly chopped

2 cloves garlic, minced by hand or on a microplane

½ yellow onion, julienned

3 bunches kale, stems removed, hand-torn into 1½ × 1½-inch pieces

2 tablespoons Mirin (see Asian Food Glossary, page 219)

2 tablespoons soy sauce

2 tablespoons rice vinegar

2 cups Dashi (page 167)

Salt to taste

1. Place 1 tablespoon of the oil in a medium-size pan over medium heat. Add the bacon and sauté for 3–4 minutes until it is browned. Remove the bacon from the pan and transfer it to a plate. Leave the fat in the pan.

2. Reduce the heat to low and add the remaining tablespoon of oil to the pan. Add the garlic and sauté for 45 seconds until it is aromatic. Add the onion and sauté for another 2–3 minutes until it is translucent.

3. Return the bacon to the pan. Then add the kale.

4. Add the mirin, soy sauce, vinegar, and dashi to the pan.

5. Keep the heat under the pan on low and braise the kale for 3–4 minutes until the leaves are wilted, but still vibrantly green.

6. Add salt to taste.

My First Job in the Restaurant Business

My first job ever was when I was sixteen years old. It was the summer between my junior and senior year of high school. I had just broken up with my girlfriend and I needed to occupy my mind and my time with a job. I quickly found a job with Silverman's at the strip mall down the street. In hindsight, I was way too amped for a $6 an hour minimum-wage job. The plan was to work the early morning shift from 6 a.m. to 2 p.m. and then go to soccer practice in the evenings. It was my first foray into the food business, and I really didn't know what to expect. While most of my friends were lying around the pool and taking vacations, I went to work. I would drive in every morning at 5:45, blasting Guns N' Roses's "November Rain" and drinking a Coke®. At sixteen, I already had a chip on my shoulder and was pissed off at the world.

The restaurant's general manager, who had hired me, was rarely—if ever—present. I didn't have a position to start, so on day one I was washing dishes. After some quick employee turnover, I was cutting bagels and making sandwiches. There was no formal training process. I studied and learned the menu items from the pictures taped above the low boys. By my second week on the job, I was already a key component on the line for the after-church Sunday brunch rush.

Despite the early mornings, I really enjoyed working at Silverman's. I would walk in every morning to the intoxicating smell of bagels and hazelnut coffee. I loved it when we got a rush and I had to make the different bagel and breakfast sandwiches. Who knew you could microwave fucking eggs!? It felt good to put in eight hours of work and clock out at the end of the day. I found comfort and fulfillment in that. To this day, I've always wanted to come home from a long shift tired. Being tired means you did something. It means you didn't waste your day.

Despite the overall positive nature of the job, there were some rough days at Silverman's. One day a woman walked in and ordered a "bagel dog," an "everything bagel" wrapped around a hot dog. After her order was taken, she had sat down, and she'd received her bagel dog, the woman walked back to me at the register. "You didn't cook my bagel dog properly and the dog is cold," she said. And then, still chewing, she spit the rest of the bagel dog out onto her plate, handed it to me, and said, "Thanks, I'll take a new one." As I stared at bagel dog spit-out on the plate, I quickly realized that in the food industry there will be days where you eat shit. To this day, that hasn't changed. My staff and I go to work every day aiming to please and serve. Some days we don't get it right and once in a while we get treated poorly. It's part of the game. I'm not bitching or whining, I'm just telling you how it is.

That summer of '99 I cleared $1,000 working forty hours a week for three months. I learned the meaning of hard work and a paycheck. And then I blew it all on a speaker system with subs for my SUV. Even though I was developing the skills I'd need to be successful in the future—arriving at work on time, getting my hands dirty, understanding others—I still did not truly value money. If I did, I wouldn't have blown it all on a stereo system. I was a stupid teenager. It wasn't until eleven years later, at the age of twenty-seven—when I went to work for myself in a food truck and slaved away eighty hours a week for no paycheck—that I truly learned the value of money. At that point, the $1,000 I had earned that summer looked way better.

BRISKET GRILLED CHEESE

Serves 4

Grilled cheese is the ultimate comfort food. Ever since I watched the movie *Chef*, where Jon Favreau whips up a grilled cheese sandwich for his son, I have thought to myself, *maybe one day I can share an awesome grilled cheese sandwich with my son.* Now, with this recipe, you can, too.

FOR THE ONION JAM

Makes 2 cups

2 yellow onions

½ red onion

2 tablespoons olive oil

1 teaspoon kosher salt

½ teaspoon freshly ground black pepper

¼ teaspoon Kochukaru Flakes (see Asian Food Glossary, page 219) or use red pepper flakes

1 tablespoon Italian seasoning

2 tablespoons white sugar

2 tablespoons brown sugar

2 teaspoons red wine vinegar

TO MAKE THE ONION JAM

1. Slice the yellow and red onions thinly, using a mandoline. The onions should be about ¹/₈ inch thick.

2. Heat the olive oil in a sauté pan and brown the onions on very low heat.

3. When the onions become a little soft and translucent after about 6–7 minutes, add the salt, pepper, kochukaru flakes (or red pepper flakes), Italian seasoning, and both white and brown sugar. Continue cooking the onions for 30–40 minutes. The onions will eventually start to turn a very dark brown. This process will take a while, so just be patient and keep cooking the onions over low heat.

4. Once the onions have turned dark brown, add the vinegar to the onions and wait for the vinegar to burn off. The vinegar should start to burn off and evaporate immediately. While the vinegar is burning off, make sure to scrape the bottom of the pan to get all the brown bits and incorporate them with the onions.

5. Remove the onions from the pan and refrigerate them for up to 5–7 days.

ASSEMBLY

¼ cup mayonnaise, at room temperature

8 slices Texas Toast (see Note)

8 slices American cheese

1 pound Dry Rubbed Brisket (page 38)

½ cup Onion Jam (recipe above), warmed

¼ cup Peach BBQ Sauce (page 177), at room temperature

1. Using a knife, schmear ¹/₂ tablespoon of mayonnaise on the outside of each slice of Texas toast. We are using mayonnaise instead of butter on the exterior of the

sandwich because mayonnaise has a higher smoke point and will result in your bread browning more slowly, giving your cheese more time to melt.

2. Next, place 2 slices of cheese on the toast, and then layer 4 ounces of brisket on top of the cheese, followed by 2 tablespoons of onion jam and 1 tablespoon of peach BBQ sauce. Place another slice of Texas toast on top to complete the sandwich. Make sure the sides of the toast that were spread with mayo face the outside of the sandwich. The mayonnaise will allow you to grill the sandwich without burning it.

3. Heat a large skillet over medium heat, then place the sandwich in the skillet.

4. After about 2½ minutes, use a spatula to check the color of the bottom piece of toast. If it has turned a golden brown, flip the sandwich.

5. Grill for another 2 ½ minutes, then take the sandwich off the skillet. Slice the sandwich in half on a bias and eat immediately.

. . . .

Note Texas Toast is readily available at most supermarkets. As an alternative, you can look for extra-thick sliced white bread or, if you want to get extra fancy, you could try a Japanese milk bread. Japanese milk bread is known for its extra fluffy texture and sweeter flavor. You can find Japanese milk bread at most Asian specialty grocery stores in the frozen bread section.

. . . .

BACON JAM FRIES

Serves 4

This was one of the original creations for our food truck, way back in 2011, when we were serving the drunk masses late at night. Tacos weren't enough to satisfy their munchies, so we had to come up with something bigger and better. Our bacon jam fries are the poster boy for exactly what you would want to eat while drunk: salty-sweet bacon jam and cheddar cheese, tossed with piping-hot fries, then topped with Sriracha Mayo (page 181) and a fried egg. Nadia G once called these fries "better than poutine." She was right.

FOR THE BACON JAM

Makes 2 cups

1½ tablespoons vegetable oil

1 large yellow onion, chopped

7 cloves garlic, peeled

1½ pound bacon bits and ends (see Note)

⅓ cup maple syrup

TO MAKE THE BACON JAM

1. In a medium-size pan, heat the oil. When the oil starts to shimmer, add the chopped onion and garlic cloves. Sauté the vegetables for 5 minutes over low heat, constantly stirring them in the pan.

2. In a separate large pan, place the bacon bits and ends, and render the bacon (cook off the fat) over medium-low heat for 10 minutes. Once most of the fat from the bacon has been rendered, pour off the fat and keep the bacon bits and ends in the pan. Add the onion and garlic cloves to the pan and simmer all the ingredients over low heat for 1 hour. You are not looking for crispy bacon, so don't turn up the heat.

3. At this point, the bacon should be even further rendered. Remove the pan from the heat and place the ingredients from the pan in a food processor. Puree the mixture.

4. Add the maple syrup to the pureed bacon jam. You can serve the jam immediately or refrigerate it for up to 1 week.

Note You can find bacon bits and ends at most grocery stores. If you cannot find the bits and ends for some reason, you can always use full strips of bacon.

You can always reserve the bacon fat to cook with or season your noodle bowls. Just let it get down to room temperature in a pan and place it inside a sealed container in your fridge.

FOR THE FRIES

1½ pounds russet potatoes, washed and scrubbed

2 quarts peanut oil or vegetable oil

Kosher salt to taste

TO MAKE THE FRIES

1. Cut the potatoes into $^1/_4 \times {}^1/_4$-inch-thick pieces, using a mandoline.

2. Soak the potatoes in an ice water bath to help remove the starch. Drain and continue to rinse the potatoes until the water runs clear.

3. Cover two baking sheets with paper towels. Place the cut potatoes on the paper towels to dry. It's important that the potatoes are dry before they hit the hot oil, or the oil will spit and bubble profusely.

4. Place the oil into a deep pot and heat it to 275°F.

5. Once the oil reaches 275°F, blanch the potatoes for 3 minutes until they're soft and browned. *Blanching* in this instance means parfrying the potatoes at a lower temperature so that you can fry them again at a higher temperature to achieve maximum crispiness.

6. Remove the potatoes with a spider or slotted spoon and dry them on the baking sheets covered with paper towels. Make sure not to lay the potatoes on top of one another.

7. Raise the heat of the oil to 350°F. Deep-fry the potatoes again, in small batches, at 350°F for 2–3 minutes, or until they are golden brown. Use a spider strainer or a similar tool to fish the fries out of the oil.

8. Place the fries on a bed of paper towels and season them with kosher salt.

ASSEMBLY

1 tablespoon vegetable oil

2 eggs

Kosher salt to taste

Freshly ground black pepper to taste

¼ cup Bacon Jam (recipe above), at room temperature

½ cup shredded cheddar cheese

2 tablespoons Sriracha Mayo (page xxx)

¼ cup green onions, chopped

1. In a nonstick pan, heat the oil over low heat. When the oil starts to shimmer, drop the 2 eggs into the pan and season them with salt and pepper. Cook the eggs slowly until you have two eggs sunny side up.

2. When the eggs are almost done cooking, toss the fries with the bacon jam and cheese in a mixing bowl. This recipe yields at least two large plates of bacon jam fries.

3. Top each plate of fries with a fried egg, Sriracha Mayo, and green onions.

Finding My Kwan & Another Restaurant Gig

After I graduated from high school, I moved to St. Louis to attend Washington University, where I double-majored in finance and marketing. College was largely uneventful. I was still figuring out what I wanted to do. My ultimate dream was to pursue a career as a sports agent. I had watched *Jerry Maguire* about twenty times and thought being an agent would be my kwan. I was a sports fanatic and, to this day, sports is one of my true passions.

I spent the summer of my sophomore year of college in Skokie, Illinois, working as an intern for a sports management company. It was a pretty large and well-respected group, representing big-name athletes at the time. That summer I was holed up in an Extended Stay America in suburbia. Since I was only nineteen, I wasn't even old enough to grab a beer at the bars. I spent my mornings literally walking across a parking lot from Extended Stay to the office.

I took a second, part-time job at Flannigan's, which was in a neighboring mall. I didn't get paid a ton as an intern, so I had to find a way to cover some of my expenses. Flannigan's was a semi-disaster of a restaurant operation. The general manager was hardly ever there (a recurring theme at chain restaurants, it seems). And when he was there, he would tell me stories of how his married life sucked and how he didn't have sex with his wife anymore. The restaurant itself ran okay. It was dark and dreary and the dining room was carpeted a dark blue. Flannigan's, at the time, was on a downward spiral, poised to fade from relevance. To me, it was a reminder that you have to constantly evolve in the restaurant business or risk dying.

I eventually found my way to law school, and, after graduating, wound up at a firm in St. Louis, which had a small sports law practice: two attorneys, who practiced as corporate lawyers during the day, also doubled as sports agents by night. As a first-year associate, I was required to bill 1,850 hours, which equated to about 35–40 hours per week. You may be thinking to yourself, "Hey, that's not too bad!" However, there are a lot of hours spent in a law office that are *not* billable. This includes anything and everything from CLEs (Continuing Learning Education seminars) to client development to just general bullshit. As I entered my second year at the firm, the Great Recession hit and I was forced to take on whatever work I could to meet my billable hours. I was handed the work that most of the attorneys at the firm didn't want to take on: products liability suits. There was no real "choice" involved in what I could and could not take on. I was just trying to keep my head above water, since I was barely on pace to even bill 1,650 hours a year, 200 short of the minimum.

The real eye-opener came for me when one of the firm's partners strolled into my office and started up a conversation about his son. His son was beginning the process of applying to college, and he had advised his son to go into business. "I don't want him doing what I do. I told him he needs to go to business school," he said. At that point it dawned on me. If I didn't make a career change soon, I was going to be this partner in twenty years, telling my son to go into business. I was only twenty-six at the time, but I felt that time was passing me by. It would be too hard to leave the firm in year five or six, potentially being on the cusp of partnership. If I was going to make a move, it had to be now.

KOREAN BRAISED SHORT RIBS

Serves 4

When our catering operation gradually grew into a full-service operation, our menu evolved with it. We created an entirely new section of the menu that focused on comfort food. Braised short ribs are the epitome of American comfort food. Almost anyone attending a wedding or corporate event can get behind braised short ribs. Of course, we had to put our own spin on the standard recipe by adding some Korean flair. These short ribs are a great winter dish paired with Wasabi Mashed Potatoes (page 90) or Nori Cauliflower Puree (page 138).

FOR THE DRY RUB

1 tablespoon Chinese Five-Spice Powder
(see Asian Food Glossary, page 219)

1 tablespoon brown sugar

½ tablespoon kosher salt

½ tablespoon freshly ground black pepper

4 tablespoons vegetable oil

3½ pounds thick short ribs, English cut
(see Note)

FOR THE BRAISING LIQUID

1 onion, quartered

4 cloves garlic, peeled

1 cup light soy sauce

½ cup Dark Soy Sauce (see Asian Food
Glossary, page 219)

½ cup brown sugar

¾ cup Gochujang (Korean red pepper paste)
(see Asian Food Glossary, page 219)

½ cup Rice Wine Vinegar (see Asian Food
Glossary, page 219)

FOR THE DEMI-GLACE

3 tablespoons butter

ASSEMBLY

1. Preheat the oven to 275°F.

2. Mix together the dry rub ingredients—the
Chinese five-spice powder, brown sugar,
kosher salt, and black pepper—in a small
mixing bowl. Drizzle 1 tablespoon of the oil
over the short ribs, and then sprinkle the
dry rub mix over the ribs.

3. Place a Dutch oven, or other heavy-
bottomed pot, over medium-high heat and
add 2 tablespoons of oil to coat the bottom
of the pan. Sear the short ribs on both
sides for approximately 3–4 minutes until
the rub has caramelized and a brown crust
has formed. Remove the short ribs and set
them aside.

4. Reduce the heat to medium. Add the
remaining tablespoon of oil to coat the pan,
and then add the onions and garlic cloves.
Brown the onions and garlic cloves in the pot.

5. Place the short ribs back into the pot and
then add the light soy sauce, dark soy sauce,
brown sugar, gochujang, and rice vinegar.
Add 4–6 cups of water, depending on the
size of the pot, so that the braising liquid is
halfway up the short ribs.

6. Cover the pot and braise the short ribs in
the oven at 275°F for 1½ hours. At this point,
check on the pot and see if any additional
water needs to be added so that the braising
liquid is still halfway up the short ribs. Turn
the ribs over using a pair of tongs.

7. Braise the short ribs for an additional
2 hours. The meat should be fork-tender.
Take the short ribs out of the pot and strain
the braising liquid, including the onions and
garlic. Reserve the braising liquid in a large
bowl. Discard the onions and garlic.

8. To make the demi-glace, add 4 cups of
the braising liquid to a large saucepot over
medium heat. Add the butter and keep
the saucepot over medium heat, stirring
constantly, to reduce the braising liquid
by almost 50 percent to concentrate the
flavor. This should take about 10 minutes.
Be careful, however, not to overreduce the
liquid or it will be too salty.

9. When you plate your short ribs, drizzle
some of the demi-glace on top of them
using a tablespoon.

. . . .

*Note I prefer bone-in short ribs, but sometimes
they are a little bit more challenging to find and
a little bit pricier for the yield (since you are also
paying for the weight of the bone). Another
option is boneless chuck tail flap. This is boneless
short rib, available at most large supermarkets.
If you purchase boneless short rib, you will only
need 1¾ pounds, since you are not factoring in
the weight of the bone.*

. . . .

WASABI MASHED POTATOES

Serves 4-6

These mashed potatoes have been a hit on our catering menu ever since we introduced them. Mashed potatoes are certainly approachable, but, in general, I find them a little boring. These, however, are kicked up with wasabi powder, and they are addictive. They make a great pair with braised short ribs or any type of steak or braised meat. You can also top them with some fried shallots or garlic for extra crunch.

2½ pounds Yukon Gold potatoes, quartered

1 cup heavy cream

1 tablespoon Wasabi Powder (see Asian Food Glossary, page 219)

1 tablespoon salt

4 tablespoons unsalted butter

Aonori (see Asian Food Glossary, page 219), for garnish

Wasabi Mayo (page 186), for garnish (optional)

Fried Shallots (see Asian Food Glossary, page 219), for garnish (optional)

1. Fill a large pot three-quarters of the way with water and bring it to a boil over high heat.

2. Once the water has reached a boil, add the potatoes to the pot and cook them for 15 minutes, or until they're fork-tender. Drain the potatoes, transfer them to a large mixing bowl, and set it aside.

3. Pour the heavy cream into a small saucepan and set it over medium-low heat. Add the wasabi powder and salt to the saucepan. As the cream is getting warm, add the unsalted butter. Stir the butter until it is melted and the wasabi powder has dissolved into the liquid.

4. Add the cream mixture to the bowl of cooked potatoes. Using a potato masher, mash the potatoes until they are smooth.

5. Garnish the mashed potatoes with aonori, Wasabi Mayo, and Fried Shallots as desired.

5

ASIAN STREET TACOS

Opposite: The wash bay at Snappy Snacks, our original food truck commissary in Austin.

During the summer of 2009, I took a trip back home to visit my parents in Vegas and decided to plan my transition out of the legal industry. I had always been intrigued by the restaurant business, and there was a deep, burning passion in me to run my own company. My fixation on the restaurant business had been tempered, however, by my dad's up-and-down experience as a restaurant owner himself. He had opened five restaurants in China and Hong Kong while I was in college; three focused on serving pizza by the slice, and two focused on Italian café–style food. By 2009, he had closed three of the five restaurants. Eventually he would close the remaining two, as rents skyrocketed overseas and staffing became burdensome. I saw how the venture had a negative effect on my parents' marriage. My dad had poured quite a bit of his life savings into the restaurants, only to see them fail. It was a sore point for my mom and still is to this day.

As it became clear that the restaurants would eventually close, my dad began to pursue consulting jobs to continue to earn money. My mom was left to help close the stores. Employees had begun to steal equipment and product. My mom even caught a female employee washing her hair in the produce-washing sink. Customer service went down the toilet. My mom was left with the dubious pleasure of trying to wrangle employees who knew the end was in sight and had zero interest in closing the restaurant on good terms. Combine all of that with a large investment loss, and it was too much for my mom. She wanted no part of any restaurant going forward.

So imagine her delight when I told her I wanted to leave law in order to pursue a career in the restaurant business. "Why do you want to leave your job to open a restaurant?" she asked. "You make so much money as a lawyer. You want to lose money like your dad and have employees steal from you?" My mom was going to be a tough sell. No matter how much I tried to explain that I wasn't passionate about law, it did not matter.

I love my mom more than anything in this world, but, as a "tiger mom," her mission in life was to raise me so that I would end up as a lawyer, doctor, or some other professional. When I was eleven years old, she would force to me to play the violin, even though I didn't enjoy it.

Playing the violin with my Japanese instructor when I was ten years old.

We would have screaming matches, where I would run to my room and cry because I didn't want to practice. My dad would run upstairs and beg me to practice so he wouldn't have to listen to my mom yelling.

My mom had already suffered through immigrant life. She came to the States when she was sixteen, and the first business her family opened was a restaurant. The restaurant came with long hours and even more unrest and disputes within the family. Her mission was to *get away* from that life, and here I was bringing it back full circle, at the tail end of my dad's failed foray into the restaurant business. From her perspective, it probably felt like she was living her worst nightmare.

Despite my mom's obvious trepidation about my new venture, I started to dig into a business plan for a Southern- and Asian-inspired fast-casual taco concept. The idea was to bring a variety of flavors and unique ingredients to the standard taco. I plugged away at the numbers, trying to figure out how much it would cost to open a restaurant. I looked at everything from furniture to fixtures to equipment. I contacted contractors to figure build-out costs. I calculated sales per square foot, and pro forma'd sales on a daily basis based on seats, guest checks, and average ticket prices. I even did a competitive analysis, looking at other budding, successful concepts in the Austin area. By the winter of 2009 I had a business plan that I was ready to push. At more than fifty pages, it was more of a book than a prospectus. It showed I had done the research.

However, what my business plan failed to show was whether I had the experience necessary to run a restaurant. As I started to circulate the plan to gather investments, I quickly realized that most people were not going to invest in me for that specific reason. The majority of my friends were making good money, practicing as lawyers and doctors, or working at hedge funds or private equity funds. They were all—for the most part—incredibly risk averse as well. Investing in a restaurant run by a restaurant novice was too much of a risk for them to stomach. In retrospect, I should have seen it coming. I really did *not* know what the fuck I was doing.

After two and a half months of peddling a business plan that nobody wanted to invest in, I was at a crossroads. I wasn't sure how I was going to open with no money. It wasn't going to happen. My sister called me and told me about a Korean taco truck that was making serious waves in Los Angeles. She said people were waiting in lines for forty-five minutes to an hour to eat at the truck. I quickly hopped on Twitter to check out Kogi, Roy Choi's Korean-Mexican fusion taco truck that to this day is credited with birthing the modern-day food truck movement.

I started watching all of the YouTube videos of Kogi. One of them showed Choi prepping hundreds of pounds of marinated Korean BBQ meat out of his "commissary," a kitchen that was attached to a bar called the Alibi Room. Since he had limited space in his truck, he would use a giant burr mixer to make all of his salsas in the cab before the shift. In the mornings, before the shift, Choi would get the truck set up, send a tweet, hit the streets, and watch the lines form. This was indeed a *movement* in LA. Food trucks like the Grilled Cheese Truck, Baby's Badass Burgers, and the Flying Pig Truck would congregate on First Fridays at the Brig; it was a giant street party.

If I was going to give my dream a shot, it would have to be with a food truck. I had seen start-up cost numbers range from $30,000–$100,000; a far cry from the $450,000–$500,000 I needed to open a restaurant. Initially I wanted to rent a food truck, instead of purchasing one. This was a similar model to how the LA trucks were operating. If I rented a truck, I could use $60,000–$70,000 of the money I was trying to raise on other things, like operating capital, branding and design, food research and development, health permits, a truck wrap, etc. Eventually I was able to find Snappy Snacks, a commissary in Austin that would take me on month to month. I decided to fund the business with half of my money and half from investors. My ask went down from $18,000 per share to $4,000 per share. By late spring of 2010, I had funded the company with $69,000: $29,000 from my own bank account and $40,000 from investors. Kris (my girlfriend at the time and now my wife) and I were set to leave St. Louis for Austin in July 2010.

BANH MI TACO

Serves 4–5

This taco, an item from the original food truck menu, has a loyal following among our customers in Austin. We serve it at huge events like Austin City Limits Music Festival. It's funny; when we started serving it in 2010, the majority of people ordering it had never had a banh mi sandwich. Now banh mi is considered mainstream in Austin. The dish is relatively prep intensive, so I recommend knocking out the pork belly and Pickled Daikon Carrots the day before you serve the dish. This way, on the day you make the tacos to eat, you can focus on the Sriracha Mayo (page 181), garnishes, and assembly. The pork belly, which is chopped in this recipe, can also be used in the Chinese BBQ Pork Taco on page 100, or you can press and slice the meat to make the Pork Belly Bowl on page 145.

FOR THE DRY RUB

1¼ tablespoons Chinese Five-Spice Powder (see Asian Food Glossary, page 219)

¼ cup brown sugar

1 tablespoon kosher salt

1 tablespoon freshly ground black pepper

3 tablespoons vegetable oil

3-pound piece pork belly, skin on

TO MAKE THE DRY RUB

1. In a small bowl, mix together the Chinese five-spice powder, brown sugar, salt, and black pepper. Drizzle 1 tablespoon of the oil onto both sides of the pork belly, then sprinkle the dry rub mix over the pork belly.

2. Place a large Dutch oven over medium-high heat and add the remaining 2 tablespoons of

oil to coat the pan. Sear the pork belly on both sides for approximately 3–4 minutes, until it has a nice sear (the color will change, but make sure you don't char the outside). Remove the pork belly from the skillet and set it aside.

FOR THE BRAISING LIQUID

2 tablespoons vegetable oil

1 onion, quartered

5 cloves garlic

5 pods Star Anise (see Asian Food Glossary, page 219)

½ cup light soy sauce

¼ cup Dark Soy Sauce (see Asian Food Glossary, page 219)

⅓ cup brown sugar

⅓ cup Rice Wine Vinegar (see Asian Food Glossary, page 219)

TO MAKE THE BRAISING LIQUID

1. Preheat the oven to 325°F.

2. Place a Dutch oven over medium heat and add 2 tablespoons of oil to coat the pan, then add the quartered onion and the garlic. Brown the onion and garlic in the pot, then add the star anise.

3. Place the prepared pork belly skin side up into the Dutch oven and then add the light soy sauce, dark soy sauce, brown sugar, and rice wine vinegar. Add enough water so that the braising liquid is halfway up the pork belly, about 3–4 cups depending on the size of your Dutch oven.

4. Cover the Dutch oven and braise the pork belly in the oven for 1½ hours at 325°F. At this point, check the Dutch oven and make sure that the braising liquid is still halfway up the pork belly. Add more water, if necessary.

5. Braise the pork belly for an additional 2 hours. By then the pork belly should be fork-tender. Take the pork belly out of the pot and discard the braising liquid, including the onions, garlic, and star anise.

6. Chop the pork belly while it is hot.

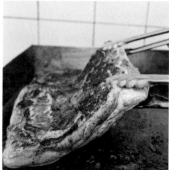

For a recipe that calls for sliced pork belly, such as the Pork Belly Bowl (page 145), cool the meat after it comes out of the oven, then place it in a roasting pan. Discard the braising liquid. Place another roasting pan on top of the pork belly and weigh it down with a few heavy cans; this will press the pork belly into a shape that ensures a consistent size for each cut of meat. Place the pressed pork belly in the fridge overnight.

When you are ready to slice the pressed pork belly, cut away the uneven ends so that you have a perfect rectangle. Slice the belly from top to bottom into ¾-inch pieces. You will then make cuts on these long slices, 3½ inches apart, in order to make rectangular slices that are ¾ inch thick and 3½ inches wide. Refrigerate the pork belly until you are ready to use it.

FOR THE PICKLED DAIKON CARROTS

¼ pound carrots, peeled and julienned using a mandoline on the smallest blade setting

¼ pound daikon radish, peeled and julienned using a mandoline on the smallest blade setting

1½ tablespoons granulated sugar

1¼ tablespoons rice wine vinegar

1 tablespoon Chili Garlic Sauce (see Asian Food Glossary, page 219)

½ tablespoon Fish Sauce (see Asian Food Glossary, page 219)

TO MAKE THE PICKLED DAIKON CARROTS

1. In a mixing bowl, toss the carrots, daikon, sugar, vinegar, chili garlic sauce, and fish sauce. Let the mixture sit and rest for a couple of hours.

ASSEMBLY

8 (5-inch) corn or flour tortillas

1 pound braised pork belly, chopped (recipe above)

8 ounces Pickled Daikon Carrots (recipe above)

½ cup Sriracha Mayo (page 181)

Fresh cilantro, chiffonade, for garnish

Heat the tortillas on a dry skillet over medium heat. Add a 2-ounce serving of pork belly to each tortilla and then top the pork belly with 2 tablespoons of Pickled Daikon Carrots and 1 tablespoon Sriracha Mayo. Garnish the taco with cilantro.

CHINESE BBQ PORK TACO

Serves 4

Pork belly pairs really well with any Hoisin-based sauce like the Chinese BBQ sauce used here. This pork taco has been on our street food menu for many years and has always been a crowd pleaser. The slaw on top offers some nice texture and crunch to offset the richness of the pork belly.

FOR THE ASIAN SLAW

2 cups purple cabbage, thinly shredded on a mandoline

⅔ cup green cabbage, thinly shredded on a mandoline

1 cup carrots, peeled and julienned

¼ cup green onions, sliced on a bias ¼-inch wide

¼ cup cilantro leaves, whole

1½ tablespoons Chinese BBQ Sauce (page 167)

Salt to taste

Freshly ground black pepper to taste

TO MAKE THE ASIAN SLAW

Combine the purple cabbage, green cabbage, carrots, green onions, cilantro, and Chinese BBQ sauce. Season with a pinch of salt and freshly ground black pepper.

ASSEMBLY

8 (5-inch) corn or flour tortillas

1 pound braised pork belly, chopped (page 98)

Asian Slaw (recipe above)

¼ cup additional Chinese BBQ sauce (page 167), as needed

¼ cup cilantro, roughly chopped

1 lime, cut into wedges

Heat the tortillas on a dry skillet over medium heat. Add a 2-ounce serving of chopped pork belly to each tortilla, then top the pork belly with 1 ounce of the Asian Slaw. Add a tablespoon of the Chinese BBQ sauce, if desired, and then a sprinkle of cilantro. Garnish the taco with a lime wedge.

KOREAN STEAK TACO

Serves 4

Roy Choi started the Korean taco movement with Kogi Korean BBQ, his Korean-Mexican fusion taco truck. This taco is an attempt to further extend the movement with our own twist. Since the steak needs to be marinated overnight, I recommend prepping both the steak and the Tomatillo Salsa a day ahead. The Peach Pickled Red Onions can be made as many as two weeks ahead of time.

FOR THE KOREAN STEAK MARINADE

Makes about 2 cups

½ cup Gochujang (see Asian Food Glossary, page 219)

⅔ cup Mirin (see Asian Food Glossary, page 219)

⅓ cup dry Sake (see Asian Food Glossary, page 219)

2½ tablespoons Fish Sauce (see Asian Food Glossary, page 219)

⅓ cup vegetable oil

3 cloves garlic

⅓-inch knob of ginger, peeled

TO MAKE THE KOREAN STEAK MARINADE

Puree the gochujang, mirin, sake, fish sauce, oil, garlic, and ginger in a blender and set the marinade aside.

FOR THE TOMATILLO SALSA

Makes about 2 ½ cups

1 pound tomatillos, husk removed

½ small yellow onion, quartered

1 jalapeño chile, stem removed and seeded

2 cloves garlic

2 tablespoons vegetable oil

1¾ teaspoon salt

½ teaspoon cumin

½ cup cilantro, roughly chopped, bottom
  stems removed

TO MAKE THE TOMATILLO SALSA

1. Preheat the oven to 375°F and place the whole tomatillos, yellow onion, jalapeño, and garlic on a sheet pan.

2. Drizzle the oil over the vegetables and toss them with 1 teaspoon of the salt.

3. Roast the vegetables in the oven for 35 minutes, until they have browned and the tomatillos are cooked through. Halfway through the cooking time, make sure to turn over the vegetables and rotate the sheet pan (to ensure even roasting).

4. Move the vegetable mixture into a food processor and add the cumin, cilantro, and remaining ¾ teaspoon of salt. Puree the ingredients in a food processor and refrigerate the marinade.

ASSEMBLY

1 pound rib eye steak, diced into ¼ × ¼-inch
  cubes (see Note)

¾ cups Korean Steak Marinade (page 101)

1 tablespoon canola oil

8 (5-inch) corn or flour tortillas

2 cups arugula

½ cup Tomatillo Salsa (recipe above)

½ cup Cotija cheese

1 avocado, sliced

½ cup Peach Pickled Red Onions
  (page 179)

4 tablespoons Fried Shallots (see Asian Food
  Glossary, page 219)

Note *I recommend freezing the meat for about 30 minutes before you dice it so that it is easier to cut.*

1. Place the steak in a large mixing bowl and thoroughly coat in the Korean Steak Marinade. Transfer the mixture to an airtight container and refrigerate overnight.

2. Heat a large skillet over medium heat and add the oil. Once the oil starts to shimmer, add the marinated steak. If there is any excess marinade, drain it before moving the steak to the pan. Cook the meat for 3–4 minutes.

3. In a separate pan, heat the tortillas over medium heat. If you would prefer to heat the tortillas in advance, you can keep them warm inside a folded cloth napkin. This will keep the tacos from cooling too quickly before plating them.

4. Place some of the arugula on top of a tortilla, then add about 2 ounces of the steak. Top the meat with the Tomatillo Salsa, Cotija cheese, avocado, Peach Pickled Red Onions, and fried shallots.

Humble Food Truck Beginnings

In late July 2010, Kris and I arrived in Austin, after driving two days from St. Louis. We had found our apartment online and knew little about the area we were going to be living in, and neither of us had any friends or family there. It occurred to us that there wouldn't be much of a support system if things started to veer off the planned path.

I had two months to get the business open. One of the first things I did was hire a chef, because I was completely focused on all the aspects of setting up the business: forming the company, getting all my investors to sign the operating agreement, funding the company, leasing the truck, wrapping the truck, finalizing our website, creating a route for the truck, hiring staff, etc. I gave the chef an outline of what I wanted the menu to look like, and he went to work.

Before we had our official grand opening, we ran a "soft opening" shift to test ourselves. I told a friend at Dell® that we would bring the truck nearby and she could invite forty or more of her friends to come and eat for free. The shift ended up being a complete disaster:

forty-minute ticket times, chaos on the line, confusion on how to build certain items, etc. I quickly realized that although the chef I'd hired was capable of developing great flavors, his preparation in general was poor. It was almost as if he had been out of the game too long and had forgotten how to run a kitchen.

He didn't prep the line in time for the shift to open or set up his *mise en place* fully, and he didn't train his line properly. If we were going to make a success of the opening, I knew I was going to have to really push and micromanage the chef, which I shouldn't have had to do, given his salary and level of experience.

I was also very green at running a kitchen. My commercial kitchen experience was extremely limited and the learning curve, I realized, was going to be steep. I didn't know kitchen terminology, like what a "quarter pan" or a "half pan" was. This was all information I needed to pick up fast if I was going to fix our problems and improve our overall systems.

We officially opened on September 25, 2010. We parked the truck in back of a bar on West 6th Street. This was going to be our weekend night location, where we would serve dinner and feed the late-night crowd. We had a great showing for the opening, with lines twenty to twenty-five people deep. Kris came and brought some of the friends she had made in Austin. For a split second, life was good. I had made it to Austin, and we had met the timeline of opening our doors within sixty days.

PAD THAI TACO

Serves 4

Six months into opening the food truck, we had some pretty slow nights. We were running doubles—serving lunch and dinner—every day and parked the truck at night in the middle of the University of Texas's West Campus. The spot wasn't great because of limited foot traffic. Naturally we started experimenting with a new menu since we were staying open until 9 p.m. One of my old line cooks, Doug Johnson, came up with this dish. Doug is fanatical about Asian food, and his imagination took him to the Pad Thai Taco, which we figured out how to execute. I recommend marinating the chicken the night before you intend to serve it, to cut down on prep time the next day.

FOR THE CHILI GARLIC–MARINATED CHICKEN

1⅔ tablespoons Chili Garlic Sauce (see Asian Food Glossary, page 219)

1 tablespoon rice wine vinegar

1½ teaspoons sugar

1 tablespoon soy sauce

1 tablespoon Dark Soy Sauce (see Asian Food Glossary, page 219)

½ teaspoon salt

½ teaspoon white pepper

1 pound boneless skinless thighs, cleaned, trimmed, and cut into ¼-inch cubes

TO MAKE THE CHILI GARLIC–MARINATED CHICKEN

1. Using a spoon, mix together the chili garlic sauce, rice wine vinegar, sugar, the two kinds of soy sauce, and the salt and pepper in a bowl.

2. In a large bowl, mix the cubed chicken with the marinade and let it marinate for 3–4 hours or overnight.

FOR THE PAD THAI SAUCE

Makes about 1 ¾ cups

1 cup peanuts, roasted

3 tablespoons + ½ cup vegetable oil

½ cup garlic

2 dried Thai Chiles (see Asian Food Glossary, page 219)

¼ cup plus 2 tablespoons Tamarind Concentrate (see Asian Food Glossary, page 219)

Juice of ½ lime

1½ tablespoons salted wet shrimp

1½ tablespoons sugar

> You can always use any leftover Pad Thai Sauce in the Crab Pad Thai on page 151.

Enrique using an immersion blender as the final step to create the pad thai sauce.

TO MAKE THE PAD THAI SAUCE

1. Using a food processor, blitz the roasted peanuts until they have a powder-like consistency.

2. Heat 3 tablespoons of the oil in a skillet over low heat. Add the garlic to the pan and sauté over low heat for 10 minutes. The garlic is ready when it has turned a brownish hue and has also softened in texture. It will also give off a hint of sweetness. When the garlic is ready, add the Thai chiles to the pan. Sauté the chiles for an additional 1–2 minutes, until they're browned. Let the garlic and chiles cool to room temperature.

3. Place the garlic and chiles into a sturdy container and add the tamarind concentrate, lime juice, shrimp, sugar, and ground peanuts.

4. Puree the mixture with an immersion blender, slowly adding the remaining ½ cup oil. Be careful not to over-puree the sauce or the oil will break.

ASSEMBLY

3 tablespoons vegetable oil

Chili Garlic–Marinated Chicken (see recipe above)

¼ cup Pad Thai Sauce (see recipe above)

3 eggs, beaten

1 cup shiitake mushrooms, stems removed, cleaned and sliced

½ cup green onions, chopped

8 (5-inch) flour or corn tortillas

¼ cup peanuts, toasted and chopped, for garnish

1 cup bean sprouts

¼ cup (about ¼ bunch) cilantro, chopped

2 limes, cut into wedges

1. Add 1 tablespoon of oil to a large skillet and place it on the stove over medium h eat. Add the marinated chicken. Add 1 tablespoon of Pad Thai Sauce and continue to cook the mixture for about 5–6 minutes, until the chicken is cooked through. Drain any liquid from the pan and set aside.

2. Add 1 tablespoon of oil to a separate skillet and set it over low heat. Add the eggs to the pan and scramble them, using a spatula. Add another tablespoon of the Pad Thai Sauce to the mixture and continue to scramble the eggs. When the eggs are no longer wet or stick to the spatula, set them aside.

3. Add the remaining tablespoon of oil to the first pan (in which the chicken was cooked) and sauté the shiitake mushrooms, ¼ cup of the green onions, and the rest of the Pad Thai Sauce. Continue to sauté the mixture until all the vegetables are cooked.

4. Return the chicken and scrambled eggs to the pan with the sautéed mushrooms and green onions. This is the Pad Thai mix.

5. Heat the tortillas in a dry skillet over medium heat, and then wrap them in a clean cloth napkin to keep them warm.

6. To build the taco, place about 2½ ounces of the Pad Thai mix onto a tortilla, then top the mix with the peanuts, bean sprouts, remaining green onions, and cilantro. Garnish the taco with a lime wedge.

THAI SHRIMP TOSTADAS

Serves 4

Stephani, our former Culinary Director and now Catering Director, came up with this lighter option for lunch. We wanted to brainstorm options for our customers that would allow them to go back to their offices and function. Although these tostadas make a great light lunch without sacrificing flavor, they also make a satisfying, full dinner with an accompanying side dish.

FOR THE THAI SLAW

2 cups purple cabbage, shredded thinly on a mandoline

½ cup green cabbage, shredded thinly on a mandoline

¾ cup carrots, peeled and julienned

¼ cup green onions, sliced on a ¼-inch-wide bias

¼ cup fresh cilantro leaves

3 tablespoons Thai Peanut Dressing (page 127)

Kosher salt

Freshly ground black pepper

TO MAKE THE THAI SLAW

In a medium-size mixing bowl, toss together the purple and green cabbage, carrots, green onions, cilantro, and Thai Peanut Dressing. Add salt and pepper to taste. Set the mixture aside.

ASSEMBLY

2 quarts + 1 tablespoon vegetable oil

8 (5-inch) corn tortillas

¼ teaspoon kosher salt

1 cup (approximately 1¼ pounds) shrimp, shelled, deveined, and chopped into ½-inch pieces

¼ cup Thai Peanut Dressing (page 127)

Asian Slaw (recipe above)

¼ cup cilantro, chopped

2 tablespoons roasted peanuts

¼ cup Sriracha Sauce (see Asian Food Glossary, page 219)

½ lime, cut into wedges

1. Place the 2 quarts of oil in a Dutch oven or deep cast iron pan. Bring the oil to 350°F.

2. When the oil is at temperature, fry the tortillas for 2–3 minutes or until they are a light golden brown. Remove the tortillas from the hot oil with a pair of tongs and set them to dry on a plate covered with a paper towel. Immediately season the tortillas with the kosher salt.

3. In a medium-size bowl, mix the chopped shrimp with the Thai Peanut Dressing.

4. Place the 1 tablespoon of oil in a medium-size skillet over medium heat. Once the oil starts to shimmer, add the shrimp to the skillet and cook for 3–4 minutes. Since the shrimp is already chopped, it should cook relatively quickly.

5. Layer two fried tortillas on a plate, so that one covers a third of the other. Spread a portion of the Thai Slaw on top of the tortilla, then layer ¼ cup of the cooked shrimp on top of the Thai Slaw, making sure to cover it evenly.

6. Garnish the Thai Shrimp Tostada with the Thai Peanut Dressing, cilantro, roasted peanuts, and a little bit of Sriracha. Serve the tostadas with a lime wedge.

KIMCHI QUESO

Serves 6-8

Chips and queso shape and define the food scene in Austin. They are right up there with barbecue, which is saying a lot, considering that Texas is the BBQ capital of the world. Tex-Mex joints have proliferated in the Austin restaurant scene, and each has its own play on chips and queso. Here's our riff.

FOR THE KIMCHI QUESO

4½ tablespoons unsalted butter

2¼ tablespoons flour

2 cups milk

1 pound Velveeta® cheese, cut into 1-inch cubes, or American cheese (cheddar blend is fine), shredded

½ cup pureed plus ½ cup whole Napa Kimchi (see Asian Food Glossary, page 219)

⅓ teaspoon white pepper

½ teaspoon Kochukaru Flakes (see Asian Food Glossary, page 219)

⅓ cup cilantro, chopped

⅓ cup green onions, chopped

⅓ teaspoon kosher salt to taste

⅓ cup Cotija cheese, for garnish

Tortilla chips, for serving

> If you have leftover queso, you can always cook some macaroni shells and toss them in the queso that you've heated up. You'll have kimchi mac and cheese in no time. Top the mac and cheese with some fried shallots or panko for crunch.

TO MAKE THE KIMCHI QUESO

1. In a medium-size pot, melt the unsalted butter over low heat. Once the butter has melted, add the flour to make a roux.

2. Cook the roux for another 4–5 minutes until you start to smell a nutty aroma. The roux will start to turn a slight off-white. Turn the heat up to medium and whisk the milk into the roux. Simmer the mixture until the milk thickens. This should take about 5 minutes. Constantly stir the mixture to ensure you do not scald the milk.

3. Add the cheese and simmer the mixture until the cheese melts and is fully incorporated.

4. Once the cheese is fully melted, whisk in the pureed kimchi, white pepper, kochukaru flakes, cilantro, green onions, and salt.

5. Garnish the queso with any extra cilantro, Cotija cheese, and kimchi, and serve it with your favorite tortilla chips.

Taking a Wrong Turn

As glorious as it was to open, the fun did not last long. The Austin City Limits Music Festival was held during one of the first weekends we were open in early October. Naturally, we were busy with the extra eighty thousand people downtown. That Friday we sold out at midnight with $600 in sales. That amount of money seemed like a jackpot at the time, since we were hawking tacos for $2.25!

The fifty-hour weeks had already begun to catch up with the chef I'd hired, and he wasn't feeling well toward the end of the shift. We had to drive back to our commissary—which was in Pflugerville, forty minutes north of downtown—to clean all our dishes and wash the truck. I told the chef he could cut out upon our return and that I would take care of the rest.

That night I washed dishes until 3:30 a.m., while the truck lights dimmed to pitch-blackness. Since we did not have a commissary kitchen, I was stuck washing all of our dishes in a baby-size, three-compartment sink (about half the size of a standard sink), with little to no water pressure. It was a solid two and half to three hours of self-reflection. Three months ago I had been sitting in an office making six figures, and now here I was at the tail end of a thirteen-hour shift, washing dishes in a tiny dish pit with no lights. At that point, I realized the food truck was going to be a grind. I had gone from a job that was more mental than anything else to a new job that was both mental and physical. On the physical side, the truck was already starting to take its toll on me.

For the next few weeks I was on a mission to open our doors and sell at as many different locations as possible. We were a food truck, damn it, and we were going to use that to our advantage. I treated the business not as a marathon but as a sprint. *This food truck is a stepping-stone to a restaurant,* I thought. *Let's get to the restaurant sooner rather than later.*

We had some long nights cleaning trucks at our original commissary.

Every day, except for Sunday and Monday, we were pulling doubles. Tuesdays through Thursdays, we would run a lunch shift at an office park and then a dinner shift on West Campus at the University of Texas. Fridays and Saturdays were the most brutal. We'd run a lunch shift in the morning and then dinner/late-night service downtown. On those days I would leave the house to drive up to the commissary at 8:30 a.m. We'd set up for lunch, serve, wash the truck, and then get prepped for dinner service. At 5:00 p.m. I would depart to go downtown and sit in rush-hour traffic for forty-five minutes to an hour. We'd start dinner service at 7:00 p.m. and serve until 2:30 a.m., until the last drunk had left our truck. After dinner, we had to drive the truck back to the commissary up north and wash everything. If I was lucky, we would be done by 3:45 or 4:00 a.m. and I would be home by 4:30 a.m.

We were making $2,000 a week and on pace to make a little more than $100,000 a year. I was working 80+ hours a week and running myself into the ground. I was already winded. Even worse, we were slowly running out of money. The chef was getting paid a $38,000 salary that pushed our breakeven to $3,500 a week. We were losing $1,500 a week, and I wasn't even taking a paycheck. By December 2010, I was down to the last $10,000 in my bank account.

I fired the chef at the beginning of December. His lack of preparation and focus for the job weren't cutting it, and the business was already on its last lifeline. The red flags were all over the place, and I had no choice but to acknowledge them. The chef was the first person I ever had to fire. To this day, letting someone go is not easy. Telling someone to their face that they aren't the right fit, or that they fucked up, or they aren't going to cut it is a hard thing to do. I try to be transparent and honest with people. I was with the chef. We could no longer work together.

As December rolled into January and February, I spiraled into a dark place. The physical toll of working 80+ hours a week combined with the mental toll of running a business that was losing money started to bury me. I was spending $4,000 a month out of my personal savings so that I could keep myself afloat (and the business, too). If I had taken a paycheck from the company, we would have been out of cash by February. I was completely deflated, and the exuberance I'd once felt about opening a business had been wiped away. I had no idea how I was going to dig myself out of this hole to not only be profitable but also come up with the half a million dollars it would take to open a restaurant.

My personal life at home suffered, too. I was rarely present, and if I *was* at home, I was a zombie. On Sundays I would sleep until one or two o'clock in the afternoon and wake up feeling like I'd been run over by a truck. Monday was my recuperation day before it all started again on Tuesday. To this day, I'm thankful that Kris stood by me during that time. I was so dead set on trying to be successful that I neglected everything else in my life. My wife, my family, and my friends all had to take a backseat so that the business could survive. But I wasn't even sure the business would make it at all.

ROASTED CAULIFLOWER TACO

Serves 4–5

Vegetarian tacos don't have to taste terrible and/or be filled with beans. This cauliflower taco is so light and flavorful, even meat eaters will enjoy it.

FOR THE CAULIFLOWER SPICE MIX

Makes about ¼ cup

1 tablespoon Chinese Five-Spice Powder
(see Asian Food Glossary, page 219)

½ tablespoon paprika

½ tablespoon garlic powder

½ tablespoon onion powder

½ tablespoon salt

½ tablespoon freshly ground black pepper

½ tablespoon red pepper flakes

1 tablespoon brown sugar

TO MAKE THE CAULIFLOWER SPICE MIX

In a small mixing bowl, combine the Chinese five-spice powder, paprika, garlic powder, onion powder, salt, black pepper, red pepper flakes, and brown sugar, and set it aside.

. . . .

Note This spice mix is really versatile and tastes great on all types of veggies. Make a batch of it and store it in an airtight container. Whether you're having cauliflower, Brussels sprouts, or root vegetables, sprinkle a little bit of this seasoning on top for a burst of flavor.

. . . .

FOR THE CAULIFLOWER TACO

2 cauliflower heads, stem removed, broken
into bite-size florets, and dried after washing

2 tablespoons vegetable oil

¼ cup Cauliflower Spice Mix

10–12 (5-inch) flour tortillas

2 cups arugula

½ cup toasted shredded coconut,
sweetened, medium shred (see Note)

½ cup peanuts, roasted and chopped
(see Note)

½ cup Kewpie Mayo (see Asian Food
Glossary, page 219)

¼ cup watermelon radish, thinly sliced using a
mandoline and then chiffonade, for garnish

1 lime, cut into wedges

. . . .

Note To toast the shredded coconut, spread it out on a sheet pan and toast it on low heat in the oven until the coconut has a hint of brown. There should also be hints of white.

. . . .

. . . .

Note You will most likely have to buy raw peanuts (shelled) and roast them on a sheet pan in the oven on low heat.

. . . .

TO MAKE THE CAULIFLOWER TACO

1. Preheat the oven to 500°F.

2. Lay the cauliflower on a baking sheet and toss it with the oil. Roast the cauliflower at 500°F for 15 minutes until it is golden brown and caramelized. Toss the cauliflower with the Spice Mix and set it aside. If the cauliflower does not start to brown after 13–14 minutes, finish it off under the broiler in your oven, on the top rack, for an additional 3 minutes.

3. Heat the tortillas for 30 seconds on each side in a skillet over medium heat.

4. Lay a portion of the arugula on top of the tortilla and then add a portion of the roasted cauliflower. Top the cauliflower with a little bit of the toasted coconut, roasted peanuts, kewpie mayo, and watermelon radish.

5. Garnish the taco with a lime wedge.

KIMCHI BALLS

Serves 5–8 / Makes about 30 balls

I have rarely met a person who didn't like a deep-fried risotto ball stuffed with pureed kimchi and mozzarella cheese. Kimchi balls make a great appetizer and finger food that everyone can enjoy eating, while walking around and mingling at a cocktail party, reception, or any other event, for that matter. They are so easy to just pop in your mouth, and the "fusion" element makes the kimchi approachable. Serve them on a bamboo skewer.

FOR THE KIMCHI ARBORIO RICE MIXTURE

5 cups chicken broth

1¾ tablespoons butter

¼ small yellow onion, diced

Pinch of kosher salt

Pinch of freshly ground black pepper

1 cup Arborio rice

¼ cup + 2 tablespoons Kimchi, pureed (see Asian Food Glossary, page 219)

¼ cup + 2 tablespoons Parmesan cheese, grated

1½ cups shredded mozzarella cheese

2 tablespoons Sriracha (see Asian Food Glossary, page 219)

TO MAKE THE KIMCHI ARBORIO RICE MIXTURE

1. In a medium-size pot, warm the chicken broth over medium heat. Keep it warm over very, very low heat.

2. Add the butter to a wide, round pot and stir it over medium-low heat, until it starts to melt.

3. After the butter has melted, add the diced onion to the pot and sauté it in the butter until it becomes translucent. Season the sautéed onion with salt and pepper.

4. Add the Arborio rice to the pot and sauté it until it has browned.

5. Ladle or spoon the warm chicken broth into the rice mixture over medium-low heat. Start by adding ½ cup of the chicken broth at a time, stirring the rice until it absorbs the broth. This is a similar process to making risotto.

6. Once the broth is absorbed, add more broth to the rice. Continue to cook the rice and add the broth until you have used all the broth. The entire process should take about 45 minutes. At the end of the process, the Arborio rice should be cooked al dente.

7. Place half of the kimchi, Parmesan, mozzarella, and sriracha in the bottom of a large baking sheet. Add the cooked Arborio rice to the baking sheet, then cover the rice with the remaining kimchi, mozzarella, and sriracha. Stir the mixture together with a heatproof spatula. The cheese should melt from the heat of the rice.

8. Refrigerate the mixture, uncovered, for 3–4 hours or preferably overnight.

9. Once the mixture has cooled, use a heaping tablespoon of the Arborio rice mixture to form 1¼- to 1½-inch-wide balls.

Once the balls are formed, roll them between the palms of your hands to make them smooth. Place the balls on a baking sheet.

ASSEMBLY

1 cup, all-purpose flour

2 eggs, beaten

1½ cups panko

2 quarts vegetable oil

½ cup Wasabi Mayo (page 186)

½ cup Sriracha Mayo (page 181)

Aonori for garnish (see Asian Food Glossary, page 219)

1. Place the flour, eggs, and panko into separate mixing bowls or shallow vessels. Line them up to create an assembly line.

2. Moving from left to right, dredge the rice balls in the flour, then the egg mixture, and then roll them in the panko. By the end of the process, the balls should have a nice panko coating.

3. Heat the 2 quarts of oil in a Dutch oven or deep cast iron skillet. Once the oil reaches 350°F, drop the kimchi balls into the hot oil. The balls should turn golden brown after about 1½–2 minutes. If the balls start to get a little bit dark, remove them from the oil. If the internal temperature is hovering around 100°F, place them back in the oil for another 25–30 seconds or until they reach an internal temperature of 140°F.

4. When the rice balls are done, transfer them to a plate covered with a paper towel.

5. To plate the dish, top the Kimchi Balls with a little Wasabi Mayo, Sriracha Mayo, and aonori.

Turning It Around

By June of 2012 I had reached my breaking point. I did not want to be labeled a quitter, but I had nothing left in my tank. I hated the idea of letting my investors down. I was pushing forward because I wanted so badly to be successful. However, my body was giving up on me and my stress levels were inordinately high. I felt like I was on an island, trying to deal with a mountain of problems all on my own. Eventually I caved and made the decision to list the business with a broker. I wanted my normal life back.

The challenge of owning any business is the mental mind-fuck you have to endure for the first couple of years. You take no paycheck, work like a dog, and sacrifice everything for the future. The food truck business is extra tough because it is both a physical and mental grind. You are on your feet all day in the dead of summer, sweating over a grill and deep fryer. It wears on you until you eventually reach a breaking point. I was at that point: defeated. A $10-an-hour barista job looked like a step up for me at this point in my life. A few bad employees were shitting on me, not showing up to work or stealing cash.

I listed the business for four months to try and sell it, but ended up pulling it off the market in an effort to push forward. Somehow, some way, I kept taking one step ahead, one after another. I did realize, however, that I needed to stop operating the business with one foot in the water and the other out. I needed to go for it, and time was not on my side. I quickly decided to make some key maneuvers to push the business forward. I asked Kris to redevelop our website to make it better. I purchased two food trucks that we would own—not rent—as assets. I no longer wanted to pay rent for a food truck I would never own. Lastly I hired a commercial real estate broker to find a restaurant space. It was time to make the leap, whether we were ready or not.

Inch by inch, month by month, we dragged the business closer to success. I wish I could point to a single day where the clouds parted and sunlight beamed down on the food trucks. In reality, it was a grind. We tried to improve a little bit every day. Instead of focusing on street-food vending, we flipped the food truck model on its head and geared our business model toward private events. We started small with drop off catering and then grew to a full service catering company. By mid-2013, with two trucks and a catering van in tow, we finally had momentum. I could sense the tide was turning. We hired more sales staff and more employees with the sole intent of going into a brick-and-mortar location and growing the business.

SALADS & VEGETABLES

Opposite, clockwise from top left: Asian Caesar Salad, Bacon Jam Brussels Sprouts, and Strawberry Salad with Yuzu Vinaigrette.

We had finally signed the lease for our brick-and-mortar restaurant in late 2013. We planned to open in December 2014, four years and two months after we first launched the food truck. My original plan was to be in a restaurant after a year of business. It turns out things don't always happen as fast as you think they should.

While meeting with my architect to create the floor and building plans, I was forced to determine early on what type of restaurant it would be. A lot of food-truck concepts don't evolve much when they move into a brick-and-mortar space. They keep serving a menu similar to the one they offered in the food trucks and maintain the counter-style service they already had.

I wanted The Peached Tortilla to evolve in the brick-and-mortar incarnation. For me it was not enough to serve just tacos, sliders, and bowls. I wanted to take a leap and push our team to do more. I decided we were going to be a full-service restaurant with a full bar. While I would pay homage to our street food in a section of our menu, I was also going to develop a variety of new menu items with flavor profiles I was familiar with growing up. The restaurant would exemplify casual dining at a fair price, and it would be a big leap from what we were doing in the food trucks.

Lease negotiation, permitting, and construction took almost a year to complete. During that time, I was forced to create. I was building a menu from scratch and had to think about how each dish was going to be executed, in addition to the amount of prep involved, and the food cost associated with each plate. Most importantly, I had to think about whether Austin would understand and appreciate my dishes. Four to five nights a week I was experimenting in my apartment kitchen. Some of the plates were complete duds; others were potential crowd pleasers. Each dish went through iteration after iteration. I brought in chefs and friends to try the food, listening to their constructive criticism and modifying my approach to each dish if I agreed with their take on it.

Between creating the menu, working with the architect, signing up dozens of vendors, picking out plate-ware, and handling all the other duties associated with owning a restaurant, I was pushed way outside my comfort zone. I was opening a restaurant while learning how to open a restaurant. I did, however, have help.

I had kept in touch with Josh Henderson, the chef and founder of Skillet. Skillet was one of the original street food trailers in Seattle. Josh and I had met in San Francisco, soon after I opened the business. We were both in town for the San Francisco Street Food Festival. I always had a lot of respect for Josh. Skillet had gone through a bumpy first couple of years and ended up with some well-deserved national recognition. They were selling their bacon jam wholesale (Full disclosure: I got the idea for bacon jam from Josh) and had built a couple of brick-and-mortar locations. I called Josh and asked him if he would be willing to help me out with the opening. He had always pushed me to open a restaurant, and, whether

he intended to or not, made it sound easy. Josh agreed to help and he became my mentor over that entire year. I asked him questions about everything: equipment, software, design, marketing, plate-ware, even sound.

When it was time to open, Josh and his team flew to Austin and trained our staff in both the front and back of the house. We were all learning, including me. I would go back and forth with Brian O'Connor, one of Josh's chefs, over how to prep certain items, how to pick up dishes, and how to plate. His advice and insight were invaluable. You could throw Chef Brian into any kitchen and he could figure out how that kitchen worked within a day or two.

The front of the house had to learn fast, too. I offered the general manager position to one of my food-truck managers, Beto. He was going to have to learn the ins and outs of front-of-the-house service. And he was going to have to learn it fast. For two weeks he shadowed Josh's front-of-the-house manager, listening to how she talked to tables, instructed servers, and watched the entire floor run from her perch, similar to a college football coach watching practice.

In our introductory meeting with new hires, I had asked Beto to introduce himself and say a few words. He struggled to get a couple of sentences out. Beto was extremely nervous, despite clearly wanting to excel at the position. I was second-guessing my decision, wondering if maybe I was pushing my food-truck staff too fast too soon. This was a big leap I was expecting all of us to make, and I knew that some people would not make it. After training, however, Beto picked up service quickly and helped make service a key focal point for the restaurant upon opening. That standard is still upheld to this day.

On December 3, 2014, we opened our doors. We had accomplished our dream of opening a brick-and-mortar restaurant after years of hard work and sacrifice. There was rarely a moment to sit down, breathe, and savor the moment. I always thought that was ironic. I had spent four years getting to this moment, only to barely be able to enjoy it because of the madness that is opening a restaurant.

THAI CHOP CHOP SALAD

Serves 4

This is the ultimate umami explosion in your mouth. A warning, though: There's a lot of knife work involved. Whatever you do, make sure to dress the salad right before you serve it. Otherwise the Napa cabbage will absorb all the dressing and get soggy. This dish is best eaten right away.

FOR THE THAI PEANUT DRESSING

Makes about 2 cups

1 cup plus 1½ tablespoons vegetable oil

2 cloves garlic, peeled

2 Thai Chilies (see Asian Food Glossary, page 219)

½ cup peanuts, roasted

2 tablespoons Shrimp Paste (see Asian Food Glossary, page 219)

¼ cup lime juice

2½ tablespoons Fish Sauce (see Asian Food Glossary, page 219)

3 tablespoons sugar

TO MAKE THE THAI PEANUT DRESSING

1. Place a small skillet over low heat and add 1½ tablespoons of the oil. Sauté the garlic for 2–3 minutes until it starts to brown and become aromatic. Add the Thai chilies and sauté them for another 45 seconds to 1 minute.

2. Place the garlic and Thai chilies into a blender and add the peanuts, shrimp paste, lime juice, fish sauce, and sugar. Blend all the ingredients together. Add the remaining oil slowly and continue to puree the mixture. Be patient when adding the oil; otherwise the dressing will separate.

ASSEMBLY

2 quarts vegetable oil

6 ounces tofu, cut into 1-inch by 1-inch squares (¼-inch thick)

4½ cups Napa cabbage, chiffonade

3 Rice Puffs, hand-torn (page 21)

¼ cup Fried Shallots (see Asian Food Glossary, page 219)

¼ cup roasted, unsalted peanuts (chopped roughly with a knife)

½ Granny Smith apple, julienned thinly, using a mandoline

¾ cup Thai Peanut Sauce Dressing (recipe above)

½ cup watermelon radish (from about ¼ small watermelon radish), thinly sliced width wise using a mandoline

½ cup red radish (from about 2 red radishes), thinly sliced width wise using a mandoline (optional)

10 mint leaves, hand-torn for garnish

10 cilantro leaves, hand-torn for garnish

10 Thai basil leaves, hand-torn for garnish

2 tablespoons Fish Sauce Caramel (page 168)

1. Heat the oil in a large pot to 350°F.

2. Once the oil is at temperature, fry the tofu. After about 1 minute, remove the tofu pieces with a spider strainer or a slotted stainless-steel spoon and set them on a plate covered with paper towels.

3. In a large mixing bowl, add the Napa cabbage, fried rice puffs, fried shallots, peanuts, apple, and tofu and toss them with the Thai Peanut Dressing using tongs.

4. For plating, place some of the tossed Napa cabbage mixture in a bowl and place the watermelon radish and red radish on top.

5. Garnish the bowl with the herbs. Drizzle the Fish Sauce Caramel on top.

> The recipe for the salad itself only calls for ¾ cup of the dressing. You can store the leftover dressing in the fridge and make the salad again, or you can use it with Thai Shrimp Tostadas (page 108).

ASIAN CAESAR SALAD

Serves 6–8

About four years ago, *Saveur* magazine created a list of one hundred must-have ingredients to cook with. One of the items on the list was black bean dace, the Asian version of the anchovy, except these little fried pieces of fish are preserved and canned in a black bean sauce. Immediately a light bulb went off in my head and I thought they would be great to use in our version of a caesar salad. I collaborated with Stephani on this dish, initially rolling out a grilled caesar for Valentine's Day service before settling on a cold salad.

FOR THE ASIAN CAESAR DRESSING

Makes 3 cups

4 ounces Black Bean Dace (see Asian Food Glossary, page 219)

¼ cup pickle juice (any pickle juice will work)

2 tablespoons Dijon mustard

4 cloves garlic, whole

2 tablespoons Rice Wine Vinegar (see Asian Food Glossary, page 219)

2½ tablespoons lemon juice

2 egg yolks

½ teaspoon salt

½ teaspoon pepper

1½ cup oil

½ cup heavy cream

TO MAKE THE ASIAN CAESAR DRESSING

1. In your blender on medium speed or the "blend" setting, puree the dace, pickle juice, mustard, garlic, vinegar, lemon juice, egg yolks, salt, and pepper for 30 seconds.

2. Reduce the speed of the blender to its lowest setting and add the oil, then raise the speed of the blender and add the oil faster until only ⅛ cup of the oil is left.

3. Turn off the blender.

4. Whisk in the cream and the remaining ⅛ cup oil by hand.

FOR THE SALAD

1¼ pounds chicken skins (see Note)

½ cup panko, lightly toasted

8 romaine hearts, removed from stems and whole leaves separated

2 cups Asian Caesar Dressing (recipe above)

1 cup Parmesan cheese

8 tablespoons Fried Shallots (see Asian Food Glossary, page 219)

4 tablespoons parsley

TO MAKE THE SALAD

1. Preheat the oven to 350°F.

2. Place the chicken skins on a baking sheet, making sure they do not touch one another.

3. Layer parchment paper on top of the chicken skins. Then place another baking sheet on top of the chicken skins.

4. Spread the panko evenly on a small baking sheet and place the baking sheet in the oven with the chicken skins for 10 minutes until the panko is browned. Keep an eye on the panko, as it may brown quickly, depending on how the heat circulates in your oven.

5. Bake the chicken skins in the oven for 45 minutes to 1 hour, until the skins are crispy, then set them aside to cool. I recommend checking on the chicken skins after 30 minutes to see where they are in the cooking process. Every home oven is a little different. When the chicken skins are out of the oven, use a spatula to remove the parchment paper from the chicken skins.

6. In a large mixing bowl, toss the romaine lettuce leaves with the Asian Caesar Dressing. You will need to do this in batches because of the amount of romaine leaves in this recipe.

7. Top the romaine leaves with the fried chicken skins, panko, Parmesan, fried shallots, and parsley.

. . . .

Note *It's tough to find chicken skins sold separately in a package. Your best bet is to purchase some skin-on chicken thighs (6-8 thighs) and save the skins.*

. . . .

ASIAN PEAR MISO SALAD

Serves 4

If you are hosting a dinner party and you have vegan or vegetarian friends, this should be a go-to recipe. The silken tofu gives the dressing its creaminess without the use of eggs. Since the dressing incorporates an Asian pear, it has a relatively short shelf life of 2–3 days, so make sure to consume it before then.

FOR THE ASIAN PEAR MISO DRESSING

Makes about 2 cups

1½ tablespoons Shiro Miso
  (see Asian Food Glossary, page 219)

1 teaspoon Dijon mustard

1 tablespoon honey

1 tablespoon Rice Wine Vinegar
  (see Asian Food Glossary, page 219)

½ pack (about 6 ounces) silken tofu

½ Asian pear, peeled, and core removed

¼ cup canola oil

Kosher salt to taste

ASSEMBLY

5 cups kale, chiffonade

½ cup Asian Pear Kimchi (page 166)

10 cilantro leaves, hand-torn

10 Thai basil leaves, hand-torn

10 mint leaves, hand-torn

⅓ small watermelon radish, thinly sliced,
  using a mandoline

2 red radishes, thinly sliced, using
  a mandoline

1 cup Asian Pear Miso Dressing
  (recipe above)

Kosher salt to taste

TO MAKE THE ASIAN PEAR MISO DRESSING

1. Place the shiro miso, Dijon mustard, honey, rice wine vinegar, silken tofu, and pear into a blender and puree.

2. Turn the blender on its lowest setting and add two tablespoons of the oil, then speed up the blender and add the remaining oil.

3. Add kosher salt to taste.

Place the kale, Asian Pear Kimchi, cilantro, basil, mint, watermelon radish, and red radish in a mixing bowl. Toss the ingredients with the Asian Pear Miso Dressing until the kale is well coated. Season the salad with kosher salt.

STRAWBERRY SALAD WITH YUZU VINAIGRETTE

Serves 4

A lot of what we serve at The Peached Tortilla is pretty heavy, so it is important for us to try to lighten things up, particularly for Sunday brunch. We pair this strawberry salad with a smoked shiitake and kale toast for brunch. The salad is easy to make, and the Yuzu Vinaigrette will keep refrigerated in an airtight container for a week. The sweetness of the vinaigrette and the cashew brittle help to offset the peppery notes of the arugula.

FOR THE YUZU VINAIGRETTE

2 tablespoons Rice Wine Vinegar
 (see Asian Food Glossary, page 219)

½ tablespoon Yuzu Juice (see Asian Food
 Glossary, page 219)

3 fresh strawberries

2 tablespoons honey

¼ teaspoon Dijon mustard

Pinch of salt

1 cup canola oil

TO MAKE THE YUZU VINAIGRETTE

1. Combine the vinegar, yuzu juice, strawberries, honey, mustard, and salt in a blender. Blend the ingredients until they have completely liquefied. This should take 15–20 seconds in the blender.

2. On the lowest setting for the blender, slowly add the canola oil to the blender until the mixture emulsifies (thickens and turns smooth). You can always add a little bit of ice to the vinaigrette in the event that the oil separates.

ASSEMBLY

6 cups arugula

8 strawberries, sliced

1 cup Yuzu Vinaigrette (recipe above)

Pinch of kosher salt

⅓ cup goat cheese, crumbled

⅓ cup Cashew Brittle (page 196)

1. Place the arugula and strawberries in a mixing bowl and toss them with the Yuzu Vinaigrette. Add a pinch of kosher salt and give the salad an additional toss.

2. Top the salad with goat cheese and Cashew Brittle.

BACON JAM BRUSSELS SPROUTS

Serves 4

Our Brussels sprouts tossed in bacon jam are a best seller at our restaurant, and the most popular at our catering events as well. To get optimum flavor, I recommend deep-frying them. However, if you're not a fan of cleaning up after deep-frying, you can always oven-roast the Brussels sprouts at a super-high heat, so that they caramelize. To bring out the natural sugars inside, I recommend roasting the Brussels sprouts at 500°F in a regular nonconvection oven for 13 minutes, until the sprouts are nicely caramelized.

2 quarts vegetable oil

1½ pounds Brussels sprouts, ends cut off, and quartered

Kosher salt to taste

3 tablespoons Bacon Jam (page 84)

2 tablespoons Parmesan cheese, freshly grated

2 tablespoons parsley

1. Heat the oil in a Dutch oven or a large cast iron skillet, with a high rim, until the temperature reaches 350°F. I recommend using a candy thermometer to check the temperature of the oil.

2. Fry the Brussels sprouts in batches, making sure not to overcrowd the pot. The Brussels sprouts will drop the temperature of the oil and overcrowding the pot will drop the temperature of the oil as well. It should take about 2–2½ minutes to fry the Brussels sprouts. Once they have turned a deep golden brown, with pockets of green, pull them out of the pot with a spider or a metal slotted spoon and place them on paper towels to drain. Repeat this process until all the Brussels sprouts are fried. Season them immediately with kosher salt.

3. Using tongs, toss the Brussels sprouts in a large mixing bowl with the Bacon Jam, until the jam is fully incorporated.

4. Top the Brussels sprouts with the Parmesan and parsley.

ROASTED CAULIFLOWER WITH NORI BROWN BUTTER

Serves 3–4

Nori brown butter is one of those magical ingredients that can make anything taste better. You can put it on steak, chicken, or even roasted vegetables. At the restaurant, we use it in Tres Cauliflower, where it is combined with Nori Cauliflower Puree (page 138). I think Roasted Cauliflower with Nori Butter is a great vegetable side dish on its own, though.

FOR THE NORI BROWN BUTTER

Half an 8 × 8-inch Nori sheet (see Asian Food
  Glossary, page 219)

8 tablespoons unsalted

¼ teaspoon of kosher salt

TO MAKE THE NORI BROWN BUTTER

1. Soak the nori sheet in 1½ cups of hot
water for 1 minute. Make sure the nori sheet
is submerged. After 1 minute, immediately
remove the nori from the water and chop it
finely on a cutting board. Set the nori aside.

2. In a small saucepan, melt the butter
over low heat. You will continue to heat
the butter until the milk solids in the
butter start to separate and turn brown. I
recommend keeping the heat on low and
stirring the butter with a heat-proof spatula
or a wooden spoon throughout the browning
process, constantly keeping an eye on
the butter.

3. After 7–8 minutes, the butter will start
to bubble and splatter. Once the butter
starts to foam, you will be close to the final
product. You should start to smell a nutty
aroma from the browned butter after an
additional 2–3 minutes. Spoon a little bit
of the butter out of the pan to check and
see if the milk solids are brown. If they are,
transfer the browned butter from the pan to
a small heat-proof bowl.

4. Add the nori to the bowl with the
browned butter. It will start to foam a little
bit, which is fine. Set the Nori Brown Butter
aside.

ASSEMBLY

1 cauliflower head, broken into large florets

2 tablespoons vegetable oil

Kosher salt to taste

1. Preheat the oven to 500°F.

2. Place the cauliflower florets on a baking
sheet and toss them with the oil. Season
them aggressively with salt.

3. Roast the florets in the oven for
15–17 minutes. Make sure to check on
the cauliflower florets after 15 minutes to
see if they have browned nicely.

4. Top the roasted cauliflower with the
Nori Brown Butter and serve.

NORI CAULIFLOWER PUREE

Serves 3–4

Cauliflower puree is one of those side dishes that pairs beautifully with roasted cauliflower itself or with braised meat, where it takes the place of mashed potatoes, grits, or polenta. I love serving our Nori Cauliflower Puree with braised short ribs. It also makes a great pair with milk-braised pork shoulder, Braised Brisket (see "Southern Fun Noodles," page 37) or braised beef cheeks.

¼ teaspoon plus 2 large pinches of kosher salt

1 medium-size head cauliflower, broken into florets

1 cup heavy cream

4 tablespoons butter

1 (8 × 8-inch) Nori sheet (see Asian Food Glossary, page 219)

1. Preheat the oven to 325°F.

2. Fill a medium-size pot with water and turn the heat on high. Season the water with 2 large pinches of kosher salt. Add the cauliflower to the water once it starts to boil.

3. Cook the cauliflower in the boiling water for 15 minutes. Make sure the cauliflower is fall-apart soft, not al dente.

4. Remove the cauliflower from the boiling water once it is very soft and transfer it to a baking sheet. Place the baking sheet in the oven for 5 minutes so that the cauliflower can dry out. After 5 minutes, remove the baking sheet from the oven.

5. Place the heavy cream and butter in a small saucepan set over medium-low heat. Let the butter melt into the cream, stirring the mixture as it melts.

6. When the butter has melted, add the nori sheet to the cream mixture to let it soften. Turn the heat off under the saucepan and transfer the nori sheet to a plate. Set aside the butter and cream mixture.

7. Place the cauliflower florets and the wet nori sheet in a blender. Puree the florets and the nori sheet on a low setting, while slowly adding the reserved cream and butter mixture until there is none left.

8. Season the puree with ¼ teaspoon of kosher salt. After it has been processed in the blender, the puree should be creamy and texturally similar to (although thinner than) whipped mashed potatoes.

7

NOODLES & BOWLS

Opposite: There is a certain zen I find in sitting alone and slurping noodles. Noodles are in my blood, man.

つ丼
きます

えり

そり

如でたて生そば

名代 富士そば

富士山もり
そば・うどん
FUJIYAMA-MORI/SOBA or UDON
Cold Plain Noodles Special
No.⑰ 600円

冷したぬき
そば・うどん
HIYASHI TANUKI/SOBA or UDON
Cold Noodle Tipping Tempura Bits
No.⑭ 390円

冷し肉富士
そば・うどん
HIYASHI NIKU FUJI/SOBA or UDON
No.⑯ 470円

ハートランドビール
HEARTLAND BEER
No.⑰ 330円

HEARTLAND BE
ビール ありま

あさり
そば・うどん
ASARI/SOBA or UDON
No.⑲ 460円

ゆず鶏ほうれん草
そば・うどん
YUZUTORI HORENSO/SOBA or UDON
No.㉒ 430円

鶏ねぎ
そば・うどん
TORINEGI/SOBA or UDON
No.㉔ 450円

特撰富士
そば・うどん
TOKUSENFUJI/SOBA or UDON
No.㉓ 450円

石臼挽き
そば粉

鴨南蛮
そば・うどん
KAMO-NANBAN/SOBA or UDON
No.㉛ 460円

肉富士
そば・うどん
NIKUFUJI/SOBA or UDON
No.⑪ 470円

天玉
そば・うどん
TENTAMA/SOBA or UDON
No.⑥ 470円

海老天
そば・うどん
EBITEN/SOBA or UDON
No.㊸ 460円

ミニカレーセット
かけ・もり
CURRY RICE(S) SET
No.⑱ 530円

ミニ合鴨ロースト丼セット
かけ・もり
AIGAMO ROAST DOM(S) SET
No.⑦ 560円

ミニかき揚げ丼セット
かけ・もり
KAKIAGEDON(S) SET
No.⑰ 550円

ミニ炭火焼親子丼セット
かけ・もり
SUMIBIYAKI OYAKODON(S) SET
No.⑱ 560円

ミニかつ丼セット
かけ・もり
KATSUDON(S) SET
No.⑮ 560円

ミニ海老天丼セット
かけ・もり
EBITENDON(S) SET
No.⑳

富士そばの ↑お得な セットメニュー

Those that know me well know that my go-to food has always been noodles. When I feel upset or I have had a bad day, I don't go for the tequila. I go for the noodles. Noodles for me are the ultimate comfort food. Noodles are a fixture in Japanese food culture, with ramen, udon, soba, and yakisoba. I was surrounded by this type of food walking the alleys of Tokyo and traveling inside train and subway stations. You could not walk around Japan without seeing either pictures of noodles or faux udon bowls inside a glass window outside of restaurants. Noodles were also prevalent at home, where my mom would cook her versions of yakisoba, chow fun, Singapore noodles, and udon. To this day, I like to curl up in a ball on my couch and dive into a bowl of noodles.

PORK BELLY BOWL

Serves 4

Rice bowls are the epitome of comfort food for most Asians. I am no different. I almost always have a craving for rice, and this bowl combines the fattiness of pork belly with the saltiness of fermented kimchi and pickled daikon carrots. The sweetness of Chinese BBQ sauce helps balance it all out. I recommend prepping the pork belly, pickled daikon carrots, and kimchi in advance.

4 eggs, cooked 6 minutes in boiling water or onsen tamagos (see Cooking Notes, page xv)

1 tablespoon vegetable cooking oil

12 slices Pressed Pork Belly (page 99)

2 cups jasmine rice, cooked

½ cup Chinese BBQ Sauce (page 167)

½ cup Kimchi (page 173 or use store-bought kimchi)

½ cup Pickled Daikon Carrots (page 179)

Togarashi (see Asian Food Glossary, page 219), for garnish

Aonori (see Asian Food Glossary, page 219), for garnish

1. Fill a medium-size saucepot with water and bring it to a boil. Then place 4 eggs, with shells on, into the boiling water. Make sure the eggs are submerged, and set a timer for 6 minutes.

2. After 6 minutes, take the eggs out of the boiling water and submerge them in an ice water bath.

3. Place the oil in a medium-size skillet over medium heat. Sear the pork belly in the oil until it is browned on one side. Flip the pork belly. You may need two skillets, depending on the size of the skillet; alternatively, you can sear the pork belly in stages.

4. Scoop about 1 cup of rice into each of four bowls, then drizzle some of the Chinese BBQ sauce on top of the rice.

5. Slice one of the 6-minute eggs in half (the yolk should be runny) and lay it in the center of the bowl.

6. Building around the egg, shingle the sliced pork belly on one side of the bowl. Top the remaining area of rice with kimchi and pickled daikon carrots.

7. Spoon a little more of the Chinese BBQ sauce on top of the pork belly.

8. Sprinkle the aonori and togarashi on top of the bowl for garnish.

KOREAN STEAK & EGGS BOWL

Serves 4

The key to making this dish is to make sure the steak is cooked correctly. It's easy to fuck up a steak, so if you get that part down, the dish will be money. We cook steak medium rare in the restaurant, so that's what we are shooting for in this recipe. Note that the steak should be marinated the night before you cook it.

If you want to take the guesswork out of cooking a steak, you can always cook it sous vide for 45 minutes at 135°F to achieve a perfect medium rare (see Cooking Notes, page xvi). After 45 minutes, pull the bag out of the water and heat a cast iron pan or a carbon-steel skillet until it's ripping hot. Add the butter that's called for in the recipe below, and sear the steak on both sides. Remember, you are not trying to cook the steak with this technique, you are just trying to get a sear on it to perfectly caramelize the exterior.

1¼-pound rib eye steak (if you purchase a bone-in rib eye, you will need to adjust the cooking time and cook the steak a little longer)

¾ cup Korean Steak Marinade (page 101)

2 tablespoons + ½ tablespoon butter

Pinch of salt

Pinch of freshly ground black pepper

4 eggs

2 cups jasmine rice, raw (4 cups cooked)

1 tablespoon plus 1 teaspoon Dehydrated Egg Furikake (see "Furikake" in Asian Food Glossary, page 219)

⅓ cup Kimchi (page 173) or use store-bought kimchi

1 tablespoon plus 1 teaspoon Gochujang (see Asian Food Glossary, page 219)

2 stalks of green onion, thinly sliced on a bias and shocked in ice water

1. Combine the steak and the marinade in an airtight container overnight. Store in the refrigerator.

2. Turn the broiler on to high.

3. Melt 2 tablespoons of the butter in a 10-inch cast iron skillet or oven safe pan over medium-high heat. Season the steaks with salt and pepper, and place them in the pan. The butter should sizzle immediately, as you hear the steak searing. This is important. Nobody likes a soft sear on a steak. Cook the steaks on one side for 2 minutes, and then flip them over. The side that hit the pan should have a deep sear on it. The steak should not stick to the pan at this point, and you should be able to flip it cleanly. Cook the other side of the steak for 2 minutes more, in order to get a second hard sear.

4. Place the pan, in which you are cooking the steak, into the broiler for 5 minutes, and then remove it. You will want to put the pan on the oven rack closest to the broiler. I like to have my pan sitting six inches from the broiler.

5. At this point, touch the steak to see if it is medium-rare. If you touch it with your index finger, there should be some pushback, but not a ton. It should give a little, too. Set your steak aside and let it rest on top of a roasting rack. Alternatively, you can turn a spoon upside down and stick it underneath the steak to allow air to circulate underneath it. Let the steak rest for 4–6 minutes.

6. In a separate pan, over low heat, melt the remaining ¹/₂ tablespoon of butter to cook the eggs sunny side up. Crack the eggs into the pan and season them with salt and pepper. Keep the eggs cooking over low heat so that you do not burn the bottom of the eggs.

7. After the steaks have rested, slice them against the grain into ¹/₄-inch pieces.

8. Spoon a cup of cooked rice into a bowl. Sprinkle a teaspoon of the dehydrated egg furikake on top of the rice. On one side of the bowl, place some of the sliced steak (about 5–6 pieces). Lay a fried egg on top of the exposed rice. Top the bowl with some kimchi in the center.

9. Spoon a teaspoon of the gochujang on top of the steak and top the gochujang with the green onions.

Note *If you like your steaks cooked more than medium rare, I recommend finishing them in the oven at 350°F to the doneness you prefer.*

MAPO TOFU MAZEMEN

Serves 4

People are often surprised that the Japanese have adopted so many Chinese ingredients and dishes, and made them their own. There's crossover between the two cuisines, which you can see in a couple of our dishes, like TanTan Men (page 155) and this recipe for Mapo Tofu Mazemen. I think that's why the two dishes appeal to me so much—they are perfect hybrids of two cuisines that I have really grown to love. With a mazemen, ramen noodles are called for, but they are served with a sauce instead of a broth. The flavor profiles in this dish are not subtle, given the spiciness of the tobanjan (chili bean paste) and Sichuan Chili Oil, but they can be addictive nonetheless. The Sichuan peppercorn powder, shiitake powder, and Mapo Sauce can all be made ahead of time.

FOR THE MAPO SAUCE

1¾ tablespoons Tobanjan (chili bean paste)
(see Asian Food Glossary, page 219)

1¾ tablespoons Shaoxing Wine
(see Asian Food Glossary, page 219)

1 tablespoon Dark Soy Sauce
(see Asian Food Glossary, page 219)

2 tablespoons Sichuan Chili Oil (page 180)

2 tablespoons brown sugar

TO MAKE THE MAPO SAUCE

Place the tobanjan, Shaoxing wine, soy sauce, and Sichuan Chili Oil in a bowl, and mix them together with a whisk. Set the bowl aside.

FOR THE MAZEMEN

2 tablespoons Sichuan peppercorns (see Asian Food Glossary, page 219) (you will use only ¼ teaspoon for this recipe; see Note)

2 dried shiitakes (you will only use ½ teaspoon for the recipe; see Note, page 150)

¾ tablespoon cornstarch

2 tablespoons vegetable oil

3 cloves garlic, minced or finely grated on a microplane

½ teaspoon ginger, peeled and finely grated on a microplane

9 ounces ground pork

12 ounces soft tofu (not silken), drained and cut into ½-inch cubes

1½ cups reserved chicken stock from Hainan Chicken & Rice (page 8) or store-bought chicken stock

18 ounces ramen noodles (preferably a thicker noodle, like Sun Noodle's Tokyo Wavy noodle)

¾ cup bean sprouts

½ cup green onions, sliced on a bias

½ lime, quartered into lime wedges

TO MAKE THE TOFU

1. Fill a large pot with water and bring it to a boil over high heat.

2. Toast the peppercorns in a dry skillet over medium heat until they are fragrant. This should take 4–5 minutes. Be careful not to burn them. Once they are toasted, grind the peppercorns in a spice or coffee grinder and set them aside. The peppercorns do not need to be cooled when they are ground.

3. Remove the head from the spice grinder and clean it out with soap and water. Reattach the head when it is clean and dry and then grind the dried shiitakes. This may take 3–4 minutes, since you may need to move the shiitakes around from time to time in order to grind them properly. You will be done when the only solid piece in the grinder is the stem of the dried shiitake. Set the powder aside and discard the stem.

4. With a fork or a spoon, mix the cornstarch with 1¹/₂ tablespoons of cold water in a small bowl and set it aside. This will function as a slurry to thicken the sauce.

5. In a wok or a large, wide pan, heat the oil over low heat. Add the garlic and ginger and sauté them for about 20 seconds, until they become aromatic.

6. Add the ground pork to the pan and cook it over high heat for 4–5 minutes. You want the pork to caramelize on the outside. Once the pork is cooked, add the cut tofu.

7. Add the Mapo Sauce, chicken stock, and cornstarch mixture. Continue to cook until all the liquid is simmering. You should see bubbles form on the side of the pan, and the

liquid will thicken. Season the mixture with 1/2 teaspoon of the shiitake powder and let it simmer over very low heat until you are ready to plate the dish.

8. Cook the ramen noodles in the pot of boiling water according to the directions on the package. Before you drop the noodles into the water, loosen them by separating the noodles from each other. Picture a ball of yarn that a friendly cat untangled. If you are using fresh-frozen ramen noodles (i.e., not dried ramen noodles), the cooking time should be about 2 minutes, if the noodles are defrosted. Using a pair of chopsticks or tongs, make sure to agitate the noodles while they are cooking.

9. When the ramen noodles are cooked, divide them into bowls and top them with the mapo-tofu mixture. Scatter the bean sprouts and green onions over the top and finish each bowl with a pinch of Sichuan peppercorn powder. Serve each bowl with a lime wedge.

- -

Note This recipe will yield more Sichuan peppercorn and shiitake powder than you need. These are great cooking "spices" to have around to add to stir-fries, fried rice, and noodle dishes. You can be more liberal with shiitake powder, as it is much more subtle than Sichuan peppercorn powder. Shiitake powder enhances and rounds out the flavors as well.

- -

CRAB PAD THAI

Serves 4

While this recipe incorporates a lot of the traditional elements of Crab Pad Thai, the sauce itself is much thicker than the typical Pad Thai sauce. To really nail this recipe, it's important to season the dish at every stage. Since crab has a relatively subtle flavor, make sure to use jumbo lump crab so that you have big pockets of crab flavor. If you do not have a large wok at home, I would recommend splitting the recipe in half and cooking the Pad Thai in two stages in one pan, or use two pans simultaneously to make the recipe.

6½ ounces dried Banh Pho Noodles (rice stick noodles) (see Noodle Glossary, page 216)

3 tablespoons vegetable oil

3 cloves garlic, minced

½ cup Pickled Radish (see Asian Food Glossary, page 219), minced

1¼ cup shiitake mushrooms, stems removed, cleaned and sliced

⅔ cup green onions, thinly sliced

10 ounces jumbo lump crab

3 eggs, cracked and whisked

6 tablespoons Pad Thai Sauce (page 106)

¼ teaspoon white pepper

¼ teaspoon kosher salt

3 tablespoons Fish Sauce Caramel (page 168)

¼ cup roasted peanuts, chopped

1¼ cups bean sprouts

6 sprigs cilantro for garnish

½ lime, cut into wedges

1. Soak the noodles in hot water according to the directions on the package until they are soft and pliable. The noodles should not be cooked all the way through, since they will continue to cook in the wok.

2. Place 1 tablespoon of the oil in a wok or a large steel skillet over low heat. Once the oil starts to shimmer, add the garlic. When the garlic becomes aromatic after 45 seconds, add the pickled radish and stir-fry the mixture for 2–3 minutes. Then add the shiitake mushrooms and ⅓ cup of the green onions. Stir-fry the mushrooms and green onions for an additional 1 to 1½ minutes until they start to wilt.

3. Add another tablespoon of oil to the pan. Add the crab and continue to stir-fry the mixture.

4. Move the crab, shiitake mushrooms, and green onions to one side of the pan and add another tablespoon of oil to the other side. Pour the eggs into the pan and scramble them in the oil.

5. When the eggs are done, stir them into the other ingredients in the pan until they are well incorporated. Season the mixture with 3 tablespoons of Pad Thai Sauce and continue to stir-fry.

6. Raise the heat under the pan to high and add the noodles. Season the noodles with the white pepper, kosher salt, and another 3 tablespoons of Pad Thai Sauce.

7. Vigorously stir-fry the mixture for 2–3 minutes, and then add 2 tablespoons of the Fish Sauce Caramel. Continue to stir-fry for an additional 30 seconds.

8. Transfer the Pad Thai from the pan to serving plates. Drizzle the last tablespoon of Fish Sauce Caramel over the Pad Thai. Then top the dish with the remaining ⅓ cup of green onions, along with the roasted peanuts, bean sprouts, and cilantro. Serve the Pad Thai with the lime wedges.

If your pan is not big enough, you may need to cook this dish in multiple rounds. That's fine. You can always cut your ingredients in half and repeat the process.

DAN DAN NOODLES

Serves 4

I can't take all the credit for this recipe because Stephani O'Connor helped me create it. Stephani isn't Irish by birth, but she's also not Chinese. I told her I really wanted to nail a Dan Dan noodle dish for a Valentine's Day service a few years back, and she helped knock this recipe out of the park.

For one reason or another, Dan Dan Noodles have made the transition into the mainstream, probably because chain restaurants like Pei Wei™ have put them on the menu. As a result, the recipes and flavor profiles of what people expect Dan Dan Noodles to taste like now vary wildly. This recipe hovers closer to the traditional end than other iterations and carries some punch from the Sichuan Chili Oil, but the noodles do not sit in a chili-laced broth, as they do in more traditional recipes.

FOR THE PEANUT SAUCE

3 tablespoons creamy peanut butter

¼ cup soy sauce

3 tablespoons sugar

¼ cup plus 2 tablespoons Sichuan Chili Oil (page 180)

3 cloves garlic, peeled

TO MAKE THE PEANUT SAUCE

Place the peanut butter, soy sauce, sugar, chili oil, garlic, and ½ cup of hot water in a blender (or use a handheld blender) to puree all the ingredients. The consistency of the sauce should be relatively watery. It will thicken when you cook the dish.

FOR THE PORK

1 tablespoon vegetable oil

¾ pound ground pork

¾ tablespoon brown sugar

1 tablespoon Hoisin Sauce (see Asian Food Glossary, page 219)

1 tablespoon Rice Wine Vinegar (see Asian Food Glossary, page 219)

1 teaspoon Chinese Five-Spice Powder (see Asian Food Glossary, page 219)

¼ teaspoon white pepper

½ cup Pickled Mustard Greens (see Asian Food Glossary, pg. 219), chopped by hand or pulsed in a food processor

TO MAKE THE PORK

1. Place the oil in a large skillet over high heat. Once the oil starts to shimmer, add the ground pork and cook it for 2–3 minutes. Add the brown sugar, Hoisin Sauce, vinegar, Chinese five-spice powder, white pepper, and mustard greens.

2. Continue to cook the pork over high heat for 2–3 more minutes, stirring it and breaking it apart in the process. You want bits of ground pork in your Dan Dan Noodles, not huge clumps. Set the mixture aside.

ASSEMBLY

8 ounces dried Wheat Noodles (see Noodle Glossary, page 216)

1½ cup Peanut Sauce (recipe above)

½ ounces prepared ground pork (recipe above)

¼ cup toasted peanuts, chopped

¼ cup green onions, thinly sliced

1 cup julienned English (seedless) cucumber, using the smallest blade setting on a Japanese mandoline

1½ cups bean sprouts

1. Bring 3 quarts of water to a boil in a medium-size pot. Once the water starts to boil, add the noodles and cook them according to the directions on the package until they are al dente.

2. After the noodles have been cooking for about 2–3 minutes, pour the Peanut Sauce into a medium-size skillet and place it over medium-low heat. As the sauce begins to heat up, add the pork. You do not need to cook the sauce for more than 2–3 minutes. When you see bubbles form around the edges of the pan, you'll know the sauce has thickened. At this point you can turn off the heat and leave the pan on top of the burner covered.

3. When the noodles are done, drain the excess water and place the noodles into the pan with the Peanut Sauce and pork mixture. Using a pair of tongs, incorporate the sauce mixture into the noodles.

4. Plate the noodles and top them with the toasted peanuts, green onions, cucumber, and bean sprouts.

> If you are having trouble finding the wheat noodles (I recommend Quon Yick™ brand), you can always use lo mein noodles as a substitute. Alternatively, try chajang noodles (see Noodle Glossary, page 216), which have a more slippery texture than wheat noodles when they're cooked. Chajang noodles are used primarily for Jajangmyeon in Korean-Chinese food.

TANTAN MEN

Serves 4–5

This is one of those noodle dishes where the Japanese have interpreted a Chinese dish and made it their own. TanTan Men incorporates a lot of Chinese flavors, including black vinegar and Sichuan peppercorns. However, the base elements of Japanese ramen are still present: dashi, chicken broth, and chicken-infused tare sauce. I use chicken feet to give the broth a rich, gelatinous mouthfeel, which I want in my ramen. The chicken broth, by itself, is not seasoned. When we plate the dish, we use the tare to season the chicken broth.

An OG TanTan men from Tokyo.

FOR THE CHICKEN BROTH

2 sheets (about 4 × 5 inches or 2–3 ounces) Kombu (see Asian Food Glossary, page 219)

4 pieces dried shiitake mushrooms

1½ cup dried Katsuobushi (bonito flakes) (see Asian Food Glossary, page 219), loosely packed

1 tablespoon vegetable oil

1 bunch green onions

1 yellow onion, peeled and split in half

3 cloves garlic, peeled

3 chicken backs

¾ pound chicken feet (see Note)

TO MAKE THE CHICKEN BROTH

1. Fill a large stockpot with water. Place the kombu and the dried shiitakes in the water and soak them for 30 minutes.

2. After 30 minutes, move the stockpot to the stove. Turn the heat on super-low, to keep the water just below a simmer, for 15 minutes.

3. Add the katsuobushi to the water, and with the heat still on super-low, steep the katsuobushi for 30 minutes. (This is the "dashi" component of the chicken broth. You'll then layer the chicken flavors on top of it.)

4. While the dashi is warming up, place a medium-size cast iron grill pan over high heat (if you don't have a grill pan, use a skillet). Add the oil and wait for it to shimmer. Add the green onions, yellow onions, and garlic cloves to the pan. Let them sit in the pan for a minute or two to char and develop flavor. Rotate the green onions, yellow onions, and garlic cloves to ensure they are charred on all sides. This process should take 4–5 minutes. Once the vegetables are charred, remove them from the pan and set them aside.

5. Strain the kombu, katsuobushi, and shiitake mushrooms from the dashi. Discard the kombu and katsuobushi and return the shiitake mushrooms to the dashi.

6. Add the chicken backs and the chicken feet to the dashi and adjust the heat to medium-low. Bring the pot to a simmer and skim the "scum" from the top until the broth is clear.

7. Add the charred green onions, yellow onions, and garlic to the stockpot and keep the liquid at a simmer.

8. Simmer the broth for 5 hours, continuing to skim the top as any impurities rise.

9. Strain the broth and discard the solids. Set the broth aside. If you are making the ramen the next day, you can refrigerate the broth. Any leftover broth can be frozen and used the next time you make ramen.

. . . .

Note *Chicken feet are difficult to find in most American grocery stores. However, you can buy them, either fresh or frozen, in almost any Asian grocery store.*

. . . .

FOR THE TARE

1 tablespoon vegetable oil

2 chicken backs

¼ cup Sake (see Asian Food Glossary, page 219)

¼ cup Mirin (see Asian Food Glossary, page 219)

½ cup light soy sauce

⅔ cup Japanese Sesame Paste (see Asian Food Glossary, page 219) or use store-bought tahini (see Note, page 158)

2½ tablespoons Black Vinegar (see Asian Food Glossary, page 219)

1 tablespoon plus 1 teaspoon Tobanjan (see Asian Food Glossary, page 219)

½ teaspoon salt

TO MAKE THE TARE

1. Preheat the oven to 400°F.

2. In a medium-size skillet, heat the oil over medium heat. Add the chicken backs to the pan, and render the backs in the pan. When you render the backs, you are trying to convert some of the fatty tissue into purified fat. There is flavor here. After 2 minutes, flip the chicken backs to render the other side.

3. Once the chicken backs have rendered some fat, place the skillet with the chicken backs into the oven. If the pan that you are using is not heat-proof, place the chicken backs on a baking sheet and put it in the oven. The chicken backs should turn a deep amber color after 7–8 minutes, but make sure to keep an eye on them. After about 3–4 minutes of cooking, flip the chicken backs and rotate the pan or tray in the oven.

4. Transfer the skillet with the chicken backs from the oven to the stovetop. Turn the heat to low and deglaze the pan with the sake, scraping up any bits in the pan with tongs or a spoon.

5. Add the mirin and soy sauce to the skillet. Turn the heat to the lowest possible setting, and keep the pan over this very low level of heat for 1 hour. The idea here is to further develop the flavor of the tare, not reduce it.

6. Strain the chicken backs, and then pour the chicken-infused soy sauce into a mixing bowl.

7. Add the Japanese sesame paste, black vinegar, tobanjan, and salt to the mixing bowl and whisk the mixture. Let the tare cool to room temperature.

. . . .

Note *You can find Japanese sesame paste at some specialty food stores. If you can't find it, however, no worries. Tahini is an option. Otherwise, you can purchase some white sesame seeds from your local Asian food store. Toast the seeds and then puree them in a food processor. You can add a touch of vegetable oil (a teaspoon) to help turn the seeds into a paste and develop a smooth texture.*

. . . .

FOR THE PORK

1 tablespoon vegetable oil

1 pound ground pork

1 tablespoon brown sugar

1½ tablespoon Hoisin Sauce (see Asian Food Glossary, page 219)

1½ tablespoon Rice Wine Vinegar (see Asian Food Glossary, page 219)

Heavy pinch of white pepper

1 teaspoon Chinese Five-Spice Powder (see Asian Food Glossary, page 219)

⅔ cup Pickled Mustard Greens (see Asian Food Glossary, page 219), processed in a food processor (or finely chopped)

2 tablespoons Tobanjan (see Asian Food Glossary, page 219)

TO MAKE THE PORK

1. In a large skillet, heat the oil over high heat. Once the oil starts to shimmer, add the ground pork. Caramelize the ground pork.

2. After the pork has been cooking for 2–3 minutes, add the brown sugar, hoisin, rice wine vinegar, Chinese five-spice powder, white pepper, pickled mustard greens, and tobanjan.

3. Continue to cook the pork mixture over medium heat, stirring it and breaking apart the pork in the process. You want bits of ground pork in your TanTan Men, not huge clumps. Set the pork mixture aside.

ASSEMBLY

4 (5 to 6-ounce) portions of ramen noodles, preferably Tonkotsu (see Noodle Glossary, page 216)

1 cup bean sprouts

½ cup green onions, chopped

Pinch of Togarashi (see Asian Food Glossary, page 219), for garnish

Pinch of white pepper, for garnish

2 tablespoons Sichuan Chili Oil (page 180)

1. In a large pot, boil 3 quarts of water over high heat.

2. Before you drop the noodles into the water, loosen and separate them. When the water starts to boil, add the ramen noodles to the pot.

3. It should take about 2 minutes for the noodles to cook, depending on what type they are. Make sure to follow the directions on the package for the proper cooking time. Agitate the noodles with chopsticks while they are cooking in the boiling water. Make sure the water is boiling! This is important.

4. When the noodles are ready, drain them using a colander, and shake them vigorously to remove any excess water.

5. To serve, add 3 tablespoons of the tare and $1^{1}/_{2}$ cups of the chicken broth to each bowl. Stir the tare and broth, using chopsticks to mix them together. Then add the noodles to the bowl, using chopsticks to loosen and separate the noodles in the broth.

6. Top the noodles with $^{1}/_{2}$ cup of the ground pork mixture, followed by $^{1}/_{4}$ cup of the bean sprouts and some of the chopped green onions. Top each bowl of ramen with a pinch of togarashi and white pepper, and, finally, a drizzle of Sichuan chili oil.

I prefer a thinner noodle, like the tonkotsu style for TanTan Men (see Ramen Noodles in the Noodle Glossary, page 216, for more information). It's entirely up to you, however; there is no right or wrong, in my opinion. You could always go with a slightly thicker noodle, if that suits your palate more. Given the dearth of fresh ramen noodles on the market, however, you may not have much of a choice. In the absolute worst-case scenario, you can always use packaged dry ramen noodles and just throw out the seasoning packet. As I said, this is the *worst-case scenario.*

BRISKET HASH

Serves 4

Hash is a go-to brunch dish that you find at almost every restaurant. It's what I call a "veto" item at a restaurant; that is, your most picky friend can't veto the restaurant that everyone wants to go to for brunch, because at least they have hash. Everyone will eat a plate of brisket hash. Our restaurant serves it, but our hash is far from basic. So I guess we offer a subtly sophisticated veto item.

FOR THE HASH

½ pound sweet potatoes, peeled and diced
  ¼ inch × ¼ inch (¼ inch thick) (see Note)

2 tablespoons vegetable oil

¼ teaspoon plus a pinch of kosher salt

¼ teaspoon plus a pinch of freshly ground
  black pepper

2 tablespoons unsalted butter

2 cloves garlic, minced

1 large ear of yellow or white corn, husked and niblets removed from the cob

1 pound Dry Rubbed Brisket (page 38), cooled and cut into ½-inch cubes

3 tablespoons of Kimchi (page 173), pureed, or use store-bought kimchi

¼ teaspoon Shiro Miso (see Asian Food Glossary, page 219)

1. Preheat the oven to 475°F.

2. On a baking sheet, toss the diced sweet potatoes with 2 tablespoons of oil. Season the sweet potatoes with kosher salt and black pepper. Place the baking sheet in the oven for 20–25 minutes until the sweet potatoes have browned.

3. Place 1 tablespoon of the butter in a large cast iron pan or carbon-steel skillet over low heat and add the garlic. Sauté the garlic for 45 seconds until it becomes aromatic.

4. Add the corn to the pan and raise the heat to medium, in order to brown the corn, while constantly stirring it in the pan. Let the corn develop some color for 4–5 minutes.

5. As the corn starts to brown, add the brisket and the roasted sweet potatoes to the pan and continue to sauté the mixture for another minute. Add the kimchi, 1 tablespoon of butter, and the shiro miso to the pan, and sauté the ingredients until they are well incorporated. This should take another 3–4 minutes. If you are using a cast iron skillet, you can let the hash sit for the last 30 seconds over medium heat to give the underside some crispiness.

Note Cut the sweet potatoes across the middle, widthwise, into medallions that are about ¼ inch thick. Once you have made these circular medallions, you can dice the sweet potatoes by cutting ¼-inch-long and ¼-inch-wide cubes.

ASSEMBLY

1 tablespoon unsalted butter

4 eggs

Pinch of kosher salt

Pinch of freshly ground black pepper

½ cup Miso Scallion Crème Fraîche (page 176) (optional)

¼ cup green onions, thinly sliced

1 Fresno chili pepper, thinly sliced

¼ cup Fried Shallots (see Asian Food Glossary, page 219)

1. While you are finishing the brisket hash, melt the butter in a large nonstick pan over low heat. Crack the eggs directly into the pan and let them fry over low heat, sunny side up. Season the eggs with a pinch of kosher salt and black pepper. Once the white of the egg, close to the yolk, starts to become less translucent, remove the egg from the pan and transfer it to a plate to keep it from cooking any further.

2. If you are using a large cast iron skillet, you can serve the hash directly from the skillet and place the eggs on top of the hash. If you are not using a cast iron skillet, spoon the hash onto a large serving plate and top the hash with the fried eggs.

3. Spoon the Miso Scallion Crème Fraîche on top of the hash, and then garnish the hash with the green onions, Fresno chili peppers, and fried shallots.

KOREAN SHORT RIB PAPPARDELLE WITH SMOKED CRÈME FRAÎCHE

Serves 4

Valentine's Day is always one of the busiest days of the year for any restaurant. While our Valentine's Day dinners are typically a little more formal since they are multiple, plated courses and not family style, I still try to cook comfort food. A year ago we served this short rib and pappardelle dish on Valentine's Day for our guests and they loved it. It is one of those dishes that just makes you feel good when you eat it. In this dish, you're not only infusing short ribs with Asian flavors, you're also pairing them with all the elements of a traditional Italian pasta dish—pappardelle, brown butter, bread crumbs, and Parmesan cheese—and then bringing it all together with a smoky crème fraîche.

½ cup Miso Scallion Crème Fraîche
   (page 176)

4 ounces fine-grain hickory chips

¼ cup panko bread crumbs

1 tablespoon + a pinch of kosher salt

1 pound fresh pappardelle

⅓ cup Nori Brown Butter (page 136)

1 pound cooked Korean Braised Short Ribs
   (page 88), shredded

4-ounce block of Parmesan cheese

¼ cup chives, thinly sliced

1. Preheat the oven to 350°F.

2. While your oven is heating up, scoop the Miso Scallion Crème Fraîche into a small bowl.

3. Fill a baking pan with hickory chips. Using a BBQ lighter or a kitchen blowtorch, light the hickory chips until they catch fire and start to char and smoke.

4. Lay a wire rack into the baking pan so that it sits on top of the hickory chips. Place the bowl of crème fraîche into a bigger bowl filled with ice and set the bowl on top of the wire rack in the baking pan.

5. Use foil to cover the baking pan and the bowl inside the pan, essentially creating a tent for the crème fraîche to smoke within. Smoke the Crème Fraîche for 30 minutes.

6. Remove the bowl of Crème Fraîche from the tent, cover it with plastic wrap, and place it in the refrigerator while you assemble the rest of the dish.

7. With the oven now at temperature, place the panko on a small rimmed baking sheet. Place the baking sheet in the oven and bake the panko for 6–8 minutes, or until it is lightly toasted. Remove the panko and set it aside to cool. (Alternatively, you can toast the panko on a sheet of foil in a toaster oven.)

8. Fill a large pot with water, add 1 tablespoon of kosher salt, and bring the water to a boil over high heat. Once the water starts to boil, add the pappardelle. Fresh pappardelle should take about 5 minutes to cook. Since you are finishing the pappardelle in the pan, you will want to cook it in the boiling water for 30 seconds less.

9. While the pappardelle are cooking, heat the Nori Brown Butter in a medium-size pan over low heat. Once the butter starts to melt, add the Korean Braised Short Ribs, keeping the heat low under the pan.

10. When the pappardelle are done, drain and place them in the pan with the short ribs and nori butter and continue to cook the noodles for 30 seconds. You want the pappardelle to be coated in brown butter, not bathing in it. Turn off the heat and toss all the ingredients together with a pinch of kosher salt.

11. Place even portions of the short rib pappardelle on separate plates. Top the pappardelle with 1 tablespoon of the panko, some freshly grated Parmesan, and a healthy dollop of smoked Crème Fraîche. Garnish the dish with a sprinkle of chives.

Note *The short ribs should be prepared before you start this recipe.*

I understand the hesitation about smoking food at home, but in reality it is not too difficult. I own a PolyScience smoking gun, which makes smoking at home a snap. However, if you're in a pinch, using a small amount of wood chips and a lighter will work just fine.

PICKLES & SAUCES

Opposite: We make assorted pickles and fermented products in-house at The Peached Tortilla.

ASIAN PEAR KIMCHI

Makes about 1 cup, depending on size of the Asian pear

This is a quick recipe for kimchi because it does not require fermentation, and yet the kochukaru flakes, garlic cloves, and fish sauce supply all the subtle flavor of the fermented version. It is very refreshing and tastes great in salads or by itself.

½ large Asian pear

⅔ teaspoon Kochukaru Flakes (see Asian Food Glossary, page 219)

½ teaspoon Fish Sauce (see Asian Food Glossary, page 219)

½ clove garlic, minced, using a microplane

1. Cut the Asian pear into half moons. Initially, you will need to make four large cuts in the pear. Slice down one side of the pear, as close to the core as possible. Then repeat this on the other side. The two remaining sides of the pear will not be as wide as the sides you initially cut. Slice these as close to the core as possible.

2. Place each of the four pieces of pear, skin side up, on a cutting board. Moving from right to left, cut the pear into extremely thin slices, about ¹⁄₁₆th of an inch, from top to bottom. You should have 50–60 half-moon slices.

3. Toss the Asian pear with the kochukaru flakes, fish sauce, and garlic.

4. The Asian Pear Kimchi is good to eat right away. Alternatively, you can also let it develop flavor overnight, refrigerated.

DASHI

Makes about ½ gallon

Dashi is the base for a lot of the recipes in this cookbook. It brings a certain level of umami to each dish. It's used in our Dashi Gravy (page 25) and as a base for ramen in our TanTan Men (page 155). You can make Dashi ahead of time and freeze it in containers. That way it will be ready to use whenever you get a hankering for ramen.

1 sheet Kombu (approximately 8 × 8 inches; about 2 ounces) (see Asian Food Glossary, page 219)

2 dried shiitake mushrooms

About 1 ounce (approximately 1 cup loosely packed) Katsuobushi (see Asian Food Glossary, page 219)

1. Pour ½ gallon of cold water into a large cooking pot. Place the kombu and shiitakes in the water and let them soak for 30 minutes.

2. Place the pot on the stove over super-low heat and let the temperature of the liquid heat up for the next 15 minutes, making sure that it does not come to a boil.

3. Add the katsuobushi and steep it in the liquid for 30 minutes, with the heat on low. The liquid should never boil.

4. Strain out the katsuobushi, shiitakes, and kombu, and let the liquid cool in the pot. Once the Dashi has cooled, pour it into an airtight container and refrigerate or freeze it, as desired. The dashi will keep for up to 5–6 days in the fridge and up to 3–4 months in the freezer.

CHINESE BBQ SAUCE

Makes about 1 cup

This sauce can be paired with a variety of foods, including chicken wings and pork belly— or you can pair it with some rice and fried eggs for breakfast! We use it as a sauce on our JapaJam Burger (page 59).

1 cup Hoisin Sauce (see Asian Food Glossary, page 219)

1½ tablespoons Rice Wine Vinegar (see Asian Food Glossary, page 219)

1½ tablespoons honey

1½ tablespoons Sriracha Sauce (see Asian Food Glossary, page 219)

Place all the ingredients in a mixing bowl and whisk them together. Serve the sauce immediately or store it in an airtight container in the refrigerator for up to a month.

FISH SAUCE CARAMEL

Makes 1½ cups

Fish Sauce Caramel *on ice cream*?! We do it at the restaurant because, as bizarre as it sounds, caramelized fish sauce is the ultimate salty-sweet combination. And it is so versatile. You can use it on top of a salad, on ice cream, or as another layer of flavor to top off your shrimp and grits. There is no right or wrong way to use Fish Sauce Caramel. You can store it at room temperature in your cupboard for a few weeks and it will be just fine. Drizzle some when all you have is vanilla ice cream and you're bored with just vanilla. The key to this recipe is the lemon juice—and patience. The lemon juice is a critical ingredient because it keeps the sugar in the recipe from crystallizing.

2 cups sugar

1 tablespoon lemon juice

2 pods Star Anise (see Asian Food Glossary,
page 219)

1 stick cinnamon

½ cup Fish Sauce (see Asian Food Glossary,
page 219)

1. Combine the sugar, lemon juice, and
½ cup of water in a small pan and bring
the mixture to a boil over medium-high heat.
Make sure to wipe down any sugar crystals
that may form on the side of a pan during
this process.

2. Add the star anise and the cinnamon
stick to the pan. Let the mixture simmer
over low heat undisturbed until it turns a
deep amber color.

3. Remove the mixture from the heat.
Slowly add the fish sauce and ¼ cup of
water. Whisk the mixture for 15–20 seconds,
until the fish sauce and water are fully
incorporated into the caramel.

4. Let the mixture cool and then remove the
star anise and cinnamon stick.

5. Store the Fish Sauce Caramel at room
temperature for up to 2 to 3 weeks.

GINGER-SCALLION SAUCE

Makes about ¼ cup

Just a heads-up: You need a lot of scallions to make a little bit of this sauce, but it's totally worth it. It tastes great paired with Hainan Chicken (page 8) and Soy Sauce Chicken (page 42). The sauce is also delicious tossed with some wheat noodles, hoisin, and salt.

1 tablespoon plus 2 teaspoons peeled ginger, finely grated on a mandoline

1 large bunch green onions, finely sliced

⅓ cup canola oil

¼ teaspoon salt

1. Place the ginger, green onions, canola oil, and salt in a bowl, and mix them with a spoon until all the ingredients are well incorporated.

2. After the sauce sits for 10–15 minutes, you will see some of the oil rise to the top. Don't worry if the mixture doesn't look "saucy" enough right off the bat. Add extra salt to taste, if you like.

JAPANESE SESAME PICKLES

Makes 1 quart

These pickles are extremely versatile and can be used to top a rice bowl or pair with grilled or braised meat. They also add flavor and crunch to sandwiches and burgers. Make a batch of these sesame pickles and store them for a week or two to complement a variety of dishes.

1 English (seedless) cucumber

½ teaspoon kosher salt

1⅓ cup Rice Wine Vinegar
(see Asian Food Glossary, page 219)

⅓ cup sugar

2 tablespoons white sesame seeds, toasted
(see Note)

1. Slice the cucumbers width-wise thinly on a mandoline.

2. Mix the cucumbers and salt in a mixing bowl and then let the cucumbers rest for 5 minutes in a colander. Place the colander in the kitchen sink to catch the liquid from the cucumber as it drains.

3. To make the pickling liquid, mix the rice wine vinegar and sugar in a separate bowl, until the sugar dissolves. Then add the toasted sesame seeds to the vinegar-and-sugar mixture.

4. Add the drained sliced cucumbers to the pickling liquid.

5. Let the cucumbers sit in the pickling liquid for 24–48 hours before using them.

Note If you can't find toasted sesame seeds at an Asian market, you can purchase white sesame seeds from a regular supermarket and pop them in your toaster oven—on top of some foil—and toast them for a couple minutes at 300°F until they turn light brown.

JAPANESE TARTAR SAUCE

Makes about 1 cup

If the Japanese ate a lot of fish and chips, this would be their go-to sauce. But they don't, so we'll just pretend that it is.

1 cup mayonnaise

2 tablespoon Amasu Shoga (sweet pickled ginger) (see Asian Food Glossary, page 219), chopped

1 tablespoon soy sauce

1½ teaspoons sesame oil

⅛ teaspoon wasabi paste, prepared (see Note)

Place all the ingredients in a mixing bowl and whisk them together . Pour the tartar sauce into an airtight container and store it in the refrigerator for up to 2 weeks.

Note If you're using wasabi paste from a tube, use only a touch of it (no more than ⅛ teaspoon) to round out—rather than overwhelm—the flavor of the tartar sauce. Alternatively, you could use the wasabi paste recipe specified in the Note on Page 186.

KIMCHI

Makes about 6–8 cups, depending on the size of the Napa cabbage

This recipe leans toward the more traditional end of things. You can make vegetarian or vegan kimchi, but I think a lot of the flavor is derived not only from the fermentation, but from the fish sauce and salted shrimp as well. If you'd prefer to make kimchi without those two ingredients, I would recommend substituting for them shiitake mushroom powder (ground, dried shiitakes) or kelp powder. The beauty of kimchi is its versatility and the many ways it can be enjoyed. Eat it straight as one of a few side dishes with a bowl of rice (the Koreans refer to this as "banchan"). Enjoy it as topping for the Pork Belly Bowl (page 145). Or, even better, puree it to make a Kimchi SPAM Fried Rice (page 22), or even Brisket Hash (page 160)

FOR THE BRINED CABBAGE

1 (3–4-pound) Napa cabbage, cored

2 tablespoons salt

TO MAKE THE BRINED CABBAGE

1. Cut the cabbage into $1^1/_4$ inch × $1^1/_4$ inch squares (referred to as "nabak shape"). Make sure to not use any of the core.

2. Rub the salt into the cabbage and set it in a colander over a large bowl for 1 hour.

3. Drain the liquid and rinse the cabbage to remove all traces of the salt. Use a salad spinner to remove any excess water.

FOR THE KIMCHI

⅛th large yellow onion (¼ cup), roughly
  chopped

4 cloves garlic, peeled

½-inch knob of ginger, peeled

1½ tablespoons Fish Sauce
  (see Asian Food Glossary, page 219)

1½ tablespoons Salted Shrimp
  (see Asian Food Glossary, page 219)

½ tablespoon sugar

½ cup Kochukaru Flakes
  (see Asian Food Glossary, page 219)

½ bunch green onions, cut into
  2-inch pieces.

TO MAKE THE KIMCHI

1. To make the seasoning paste, pulse the onion, garlic cloves, ginger, fish sauce, salted shrimp, and sugar in a food processor.

2. Transfer the paste to a bowl and mix in the kochukaru flakes. Set the seasoning paste aside for 15 minutes so the flavors can develop.

3. Add the green onions, seasoning paste, and brined cabbage to a large bowl and mix thoroughly to combine all the ingredients.

4. Pack the mixture tightly into 16-ounce mason jars. Add $^1/_4$ cup water to the mixing bowl and swirl the water around to collect any remaining seasoning paste.

5. Add the water evenly to the mason jars and cover them tightly.

6. Set the jars aside for 3 days at room temperature.

7. Refrigerate and consume the Kimchi within 6 months.

MISO CARAMEL

Makes about 2 cups

Another sweet and salty combo, Miso Caramel is great on top of a sweet breakfast (think pancakes, waffles, French toast) or as a dessert option on top of ice cream.

¾ cup sugar

1 teaspoon lemon juice

1½ cups heavy cream

2 tablespoons Shiro Miso (white soybean paste) (see Asian Food Glossary, page 219)

1. Place the sugar, ¼ cup of water, and the lemon juice in a small pan over medium-high heat. Stir the sugar and water lightly with a heat-proof spatula.

2. Without additional stirring, bring the mixture to a boil. Wipe down any sugar crystals on the sides with a wet pastry brush.

3. Let the mixture simmer over very low heat undisturbed until it turns a deep amber color. This should take about 35 minutes. Remove the pan from the heat.

4. Once the pan is off the heat, slowly pour the cream into the pan. If the caramel seizes up and hardens, put the pan back on the stovetop over low heat and whisk the caramel mixture until the texture smoothens and is creamy again.

5. Add the shiro miso to the pan and slowly whisk it into the mixture, until it is well incorporated.

6. Pour the Miso Caramel into a heat-proof bowl and let it cool, uncovered, in the refrigerator. The Miso Caramel will store in an airtight container for up to 1 week.

MISO SCALLION CRÈME FRAÎCHE

Makes 2 cups

This crème fraîche is whipped, which makes it airier than the store-bought version, and I actually prefer the texture. Crème fraîche is extremely versatile. Schmear it on breakfast toast with a fried egg and some sautéed vegetables in the morning or put a little on top of your favorite pasta dish, like Korean Short Rib Pappardelle (page 162).

1 cup store-bought crème fraîche

½ tablespoon Shiro Miso (white soybean paste) (see Asian Food Glossary, page 219)

⅓ cup green onions, chopped

1 teaspoon lemon juice

Pinch of kosher salt

1. In a small mixing bowl, whisk the crème fraîche, shiro miso, green onions, lemon juice, and kosher salt.

2. Place the mixture into an airtight container in the fridge. Refrigerate for an hour to tighten up the crème fraîche. The crème fraîche will store in the refrigerator for up to 5 days.

PEACH BBQ SAUCE

Makes about 2¼ cups

Everybody loves a good barbecue sauce. This one is no frills and easy to make, and our guests love it. We came up with this recipe before we had a commissary kitchen and had to cook everything on the truck. We needed a sauce that we could easily make with little storage space and without even a burner (we had to cook it in a saucepan on top of a flat top).

2 tablespoons vegetable oil

¾ cup yellow onion, cut in large chunks

¾ cup peach preserves

3 cups tomato ketchup

2 teaspoons freshly ground black pepper

1. Place the oil in a medium-size pot over medium heat. Once the oil is hot, add the yellow onions.

2. Sauté the onion chunks for 4–5 minutes until they start to become translucent.

3. Add the peach preserves and continue to cook them together with the onions for 5 minutes, until the preserves start to thicken.

4. Add the ketchup to the pot.

5. Turn the heat down to low and simmer the sauce uncovered for 1 hour, stirring it every 5 minutes or so.

6. Add the black pepper and simmer the sauce, stirring it occasionally, for 1 hour and 15 minutes over very low heat.

7. Strain the sauce using a fine mesh strainer to remove the onions. Pour the sauce into a heat-proof, airtight container and refrigerate it overnight. The sauce will store for up to a month refrigerated.

PEACH PICKLED RED ONIONS

Makes 1 quart

The aromatics and peach tea in this recipe really help infuse the red onions with flavor. We like to use them in the restaurant, not only for their great flavor, but for their appearance as well—they look great on top of a dish. If you're cooking for guests, sprinkle some on top of a robust, savory dish that has a high fat content. It will taste fantastic.

1 bag of peach tea

½ cup Rice Wine Vinegar (see Asian Food Glossary, page 219)

2 tablespoons sugar

½ tablespoon salt

1 red onion, julienned

2 pods Star Anise (see Asian Food Glossary, page 219)

2 cloves garlic

2 bay leaves

1 Thai Chili (see Asian Food Glossary, page 219)

1. Bring 1 cup of water to a boil in a small saucepan. Steep the tea bag in the water, according to the directions on the bag.

2. Add the rice wine vinegar, sugar, and salt to the saucepan until the sugar and salt have dissolved, and then let the mixture rest for 5 minutes.

3. Place the red onions, star anise, garlic cloves, bay leaves, and Thai chili in 16-ounce mason jars. Add the pickling liquid to the mason jars and secure the lids tightly.

PICKLED DAIKON CARROTS

Makes ½ quart

Pickled Daikon Carrots are the perfect addition to a rice bowl, sandwich, or taco. I like to pair them with a rich protein that is high in fat. Or, you can just begin a meal with them and pair them with a variety of other pickles.

¼ pound carrots, peeled and julienned using a mandoline on the smallest blade setting

¼ pound daikon radish, peeled and julienned using a mandoline on the smallest blade setting

1½ tablespoons granulated sugar

1¼ tablespoons Rice Wine Vinegar (see Asian Food Glossary, page 219)

1 tablespoon Chili Garlic Sauce (see Asian Food Glossary, page 219)

½ tablespoon Fish Sauce (see Asian Food Glossary, page 219)

In a mixing bowl, toss the carrots, daikon, sugar, vinegar, chili garlic sauce, and fish sauce. Let the mixture sit and rest for a couple of hours.

SICHUAN CHILI OIL

Makes 2 cups

You can always buy chili oil at an Asian food store, if you are in a pinch, but this homemade version is much more flavorful. It does take a little bit of time to make, but the chili oil should last you a while, and it's a great condiment to have around.

¼ cup Sichuan peppercorns
  (see Asian Food Glossary, page 219)

1 stick cinnamon

3 pieces of whole Star Anise
  (see Asian Food Glossary, page 219)

2 bay leaves

2 cups vegetable oil

1 cup crushed red pepper flakes

1. Place the Sichuan peppercorns, cinnamon stick, star anise, bay leaves, and oil into a small pot.

2. Over medium-low heat, bring the oil mixture to 325°F, using a high-temperature thermometer or a candy thermometer, and then turn off the heat.

3. Wait 6–7 minutes for the aromatic spices to infuse the oil.

4. Add the crushed red pepper flakes to the pot and allow them to steep in the hot oil. It should start to give off a fragrance—almost like popcorn.

5. Strain the oil and pour it into a heat-proof container. Allow the oil to cool, uncovered, in the refrigerator. Once the oil has cooled, put a lid on the container and store it at room temperature for up to 3 months.

SRIRACHA MAYO

Makes 1¼ cups

I'm not sure you can ever go wrong with Sriracha Mayo. Eight years ago, when we started the food truck, it was considered more of a "far out" condiment for hipsters than it is now. These days you can find Sriracha Mayo everywhere. We put it on our Banh Mi Taco (page 97), but there's no reason you can't put it on sandwiches and burgers—or dip your fries in it. You honestly can't go wrong with this mayo.

1 cup mayonnaise

¼ cup Sriracha Sauce
  (see Asian Food Glossary, page 219)

½ teaspoon lemon juice

½ teaspoon Rice Wine Vinegar
  (see Asian Food Glossary, page 219)

Heavy pinch of salt

Place all the ingredients in bowl, and whisk them together until they are well incorporated. Pour the mayo into an airtight container and store it in the refrigerator for up to a month.

THAI CHILI DIPPING SAUCE

Makes about 2 cups

Everybody knows mae ploy, the Thai chili sauce you can find on the shelves of most supermarkets these days. Our Thai Chili Dipping Sauce raises the standard of this popular sauce a bit more with an extra kick from serrano chili peppers and gochujang. It pairs beautifully with fried foods, like savory spring rolls, Mom's Shrimp Toast (page 40) and pan-seared dumplings.

1 tablespoon canola oil

2 serrano chili peppers, seeded and diced

3 cloves garlic, minced

⅔ cup Rice Wine Vinegar (see Asian Food Glossary, page 219)

1 tablespoon Gochujang (see Asian Food Glossary, page 219)

⅔ cup sugar

1⅓ tablespoons lime juice

1⅓ tablespoons Fish Sauce (see Asian Food Glossary, page 219)

1½ tablespoons cornstarch slurry (mix 1½ tablespoons cornstarch with 3 tablespoons water)

1 teaspoon salt

1. Heat the oil in a small saucepan over low heat. Add the serrano peppers and garlic cloves, and sauté the mixture for 4 minutes until it becomes aromatic.

2. Raise the heat to medium and add the vinegar, gochujang, sugar, and ⅔ cup of water to the pan. Bring the mixture to a simmer.

3. Add the lime juice and fish sauce and bring the mixture back to a simmer.

4. Add the cornstarch slurry to the mixture until it thickens to the consistency of a thick salad dressing (it should not be liquidy). To ensure that the slurry thickens the sauce, you need to bring the mixture to a simmer (you'll see bubbles forming on the side of the pan) for 15–20 seconds.

5. Whisk the salt into the sauce.

6. Pour the sauce into a heat-proof container and then place the container in an ice water bath to cool the sauce. Once the sauce has cooled, place a lid on the container and store it in the refrigerator. The sauce will store for up to 10–14 days.

TOMATILLO SALSA

Makes about 2½ cups

This salsa recipe was written by one of my longtime and loyal prep cooks turned kitchen manager, Enrique. It's a versatile salsa that we use both on breakfast and lunch tacos. It's simple and straightforward to make.

1 pound tomatillos, husk removed

½ small yellow onion, quartered

1 jalapeño chile, stem removed and seeded

2 cloves garlic

2 tablespoons vegetable oil

1¾ teaspoon salt

½ teaspoon cumin

½ cup cilantro, roughly chopped, bottom stems removed

1. Preheat the oven to 375°F and place the whole tomatillos, yellow onion, jalapeño, and garlic on a baking sheet.

2. Drizzle the oil over the vegetables and toss them with 1 teaspoon of the salt.

3. Roast the vegetables in the oven for 35 minutes, until they have browned and the tomatillos are cooked through. Halfway through the cooking time, make sure to turn over the vegetables and rotate the baking sheet (to ensure even roasting).

4. Move the vegetable mixture into a food processor and add the cumin, cilantro, and remaining ¾ teaspoon of salt. Puree the ingredients in a food processor and refrigerate the marinade.

TOMATO JAM

Makes 1 pint

Our Tomato Jam is really versatile. It is great paired with braised meats or in a sandwich, and it also makes a welcome addition to a crostini bar or a charcuterie plate.

1 pound Roma tomatoes, roughly chopped

¾ cup yellow onion, peeled and roughly chopped

2 cloves garlic

½ teaspoon kosher salt

½ teaspoon freshly ground black pepper

Zest of ⅓ lime

1½ tablespoons lime juice

⅓ cup sugar

¼ teaspoon ground cinnamon

¼ teaspoon ground allspice

Pinch of ground cumin

½ tablespoon red pepper flakes

½ cup fire-roasted tomatoes, drained

1. Combine the Roma tomatoes, onion, garlic, salt, and black pepper in a medium-size pot, and sauté them for 20–25 minutes, until the onions and tomatoes break down.

2. Add the lime zest, lime juice, sugar, cinnamon, allspice, cumin, and red pepper flakes to the sautéed mixture.

3. Simmer the mixture over low heat for 30 minutes to incorporate the ingredients.

4. Turn off the heat. Add the fire-roasted tomatoes to the pot and stir them in.

5. Using a fine-mesh strainer, strain the liquid from the mixture and discard the liquid.

6. Puree the remaining ingredients, and then pour them into a heat-proof container. Set the container in an ice bath for 30 minutes to cool the Tomato Jam. Remove the container, secure it with a lid, and place it in the refrigerator overnight. The tomato jam can last up to 4–5 days refrigerated.

TONKATSU SAUCE

Makes about 2 cups

This Japanese sauce is part tart, part sweet, and it's meant to be eaten with tonkatsu (fried Japanese pork cutlet). It produces a sauce that is slightly thicker than the Bulldog Tonkatsu Sauce you can find in most Japanese grocery stores, since it contains a little more ketchup. Tonkatsu is typically served with finely shredded cabbage that you bathe in the sauce. In my world, it tastes damn good on a hot dog, too.

1½ cups tomato ketchup

⅓ cup soy sauce

3 tablespoons Worcestershire sauce

⅔ cup brown sugar

½ cup sugar

½ teaspoon garlic powder

½ teaspoon freshly ground black pepper

1½ tablespoons cornstarch slurry
(mix ¾ tablespoon cornstarch with
¾ tablespoon cold water)

1. Place all the ingredients in a small saucepot and stir them together.

2. Place the saucepan on the stovetop and bring the mixture to a boil.

3. Once the mixture starts to boil, turn the heat down to a simmer.

4. Simmer the mixture for 40 minutes. Do not overcook the mixture and let it reduce too much or the resulting sauce will be too salty.

5. Store the Tonkatsu Sauce in an airtight container in the refrigerator for 4–5 days.

WASABI MAYO

Makes 1½ cups

Wasabi Mayo (like Sriracha Mayo, page 181) has become mainstream enough that you might find it premade at your local supermarket, rather than having to hunt it down at an Asian food store. This recipe tastes much better, though, than the store-bought condiment.

1 cup mayonnaise

2 tablespoons Dijon mustard

2 tablespoons honey

3 tablespoons prepared wasabi paste (see Note)

¾ tablespoon lime juice

½ teaspoon sesame oil

Place all the ingredients in a mixing bowl and whisk them together. Store the mayo in an airtight container in the refrigerator for up to a month.

Note If you are using wasabi powder, mix it with cold water to create a paste. The strength of the wasabi paste is the biggest variable in this recipe. The stronger the paste, the stronger the mayo. After you've made the paste, taste it to make sure it's not overpowering. I recommend using a ratio of 1 teaspoon of wasabi powder to 1 teaspoon of cold water.

9

SWEETS

Opposite, clockwise from top left: Banana Nutella Spring Rolls, Matcha Mousse, and Asian Movie Night.

grew up in a country absolutely infatuated with desserts. Everywhere you turned in Japan you would see ice cream vending machines, soft serve stores, and a ton of pastry shops, where you would always find a crowd snacking. The Japanese love French pastries and they love sweets in general. My desserts tend to mimic the Japanese approach: they're cerebral, not too sweet, and tasty. You'll find that these recipes while unique are not so cloyingly sugary that you'll have trouble falling asleep at night.

ASIAN MOVIE NIGHT

Serves 4

When we opened up the restaurant in 2014, we struggled to come up with dessert ideas that would not require a ton of prep time in the kitchen. Our menu was already so prep-intensive that we had to offer desserts that cross-utilized other prepped items that we already had in-house. Brian O'Connor threw out the idea of using Sweet Soy Sauce on top of ice cream. I tasted it, but it was too funky for me. I proposed the idea of Fish Sauce Caramel and rice puffs. Strangely enough, we both agreed it worked.

At the restaurant, we use popcorn ice cream, from a great local ice cream store, for this dessert. When you make it at home, vanilla bean ice cream will work just as well. The salty and umami flavor of Fish Sauce Caramel, paired with the texture of the rice puffs, makes this an amazing dessert. It's even better, of course, while you're watching an Asian movie.

1 pint high-quality vanilla bean ice cream

¼ cup Fish Sauce Caramel (page 168)

3 rice puffs (see Note, page 21) hand-crushed

1. Scoop the vanilla bean ice cream into individual serving bowls.

2. Using a spoon, drizzle Fish Sauce Caramel on top of each scoop of ice cream. It's okay to be liberal with the caramel.

3. Top the ice cream with a sprinkle of crushed rice puffs.

> **If the idea of Fish Sauce Caramel scares you, you can always use Miso Caramel (page 175) as a substitute. You're not going to get the umaminess from the fermented anchovies in the Fish Sauce, but you're still going to get the salty-sweet combo from the miso.**

SINGAPORE FLING

Serves 4

When I was a kid, one of my favorite desserts was called *sago gula melaka*. I ate it every time I went to Singapore with my family. It's a relatively simple, straightforward dessert, but there is something magical about sweetened coconut milk paired with tapioca pearls. Traditional recipes for *sago gula melaka* infuse the coconut milk with pandan leaves, but, since they are difficult to source in the United States, I have not included them in the recipe.

FOR THE COCONUT TAPIOCA

¾ cup palm sugar

2 cups tapioca pearls

1 cup coconut milk

TO MAKE THE COCONUT TAPIOCA

1. To prepare the palm sugar syrup, melt the palm sugar in ½ cup of water over medium heat in a small saucepan. Once the sugar has dissolved into the water, remove the syrup from the heat and set it aside.

2. In a medium-size pot, bring 5 quarts of water to a boil. Add the tapioca pearls to the boiling water and stir the mixture frequently until all of the tapioca pearls are translucent. This can take up to 30 minutes depending on the size of the tapioca. Using a fine mesh strainer, strain off all the liquid and run the cooked pearls under cold water to keep them from cooking any further.

3. Transfer the tapioca pearls to a mixing bowl and add the coconut milk and palm sugar syrup to keep the pearls from sticking together. If you are making this dessert ahead of time, and are refrigerating the tapioca mixture until you need it, make sure to have additional coconut milk on hand to help thin the tapioca once you take it out of the fridge. The tapioca will thicken while it is refrigerated.

ASSEMBLY

½ Asian pear, diced into small pieces

¼ teaspoon lime zest

Spoon the tapioca into serving bowls and scatter the diced Asian pear and lime zest on top.

MATCHA MOUSSE

Serves 4–6

When I went back to Japan again with my wife, on our honeymoon, I was reminded of how much matcha the Japanese consume. We saw it all over the convenience stores—in all kinds of candy bars, chocolates, ice creams—you name it. We also saw matcha infused in a wide range of pastries, which, incidentally, the Japanese love. (The pastry section in the Dean & DeLuca store in Tokyo is a sight to behold.) So matcha seemed like a natural product for us to use in one of our desserts. This mousse recipe is a great dessert when you're hosting a dinner party and want to impress your guests. I'm a sucker for sweets and probably could eat a bowl of this every night.

FOR THE MOUSSE

2½ cups white chocolate

¼ cup + 1 quart heavy whipping cream

1½ tablespoons matcha powder

5 eggs

TO MAKE THE MOUSSE

1. Set up a double boiler large enough to accommodate a large mixing bowl.

2. Add the white chocolate and ¼ cup heavy whipping cream to the mixing bowl. Set the bowl atop the double boiler and stir the mixture frequently until all the chocolate has melted and combined thoroughly with the cream.

3. While the white chocolate is melting, brew the matcha powder in ½ cup of hot water. Cool the tea by placing it in the fridge.

4. Continue to keep an eye on the white chocolate and whipping cream, stirring the mixture frequently. While the chocolate is melting and the matcha is brewing, whip the remaining quart of whipping cream with the matcha tea in a stand mixer, using the whisk attachment. Whip the cream until soft peaks form.

5. When the white chocolate mixture has melted and been fully combined, remove it from the heat. Crack the eggs into the white chocolate and combine the two slowly, folding in the eggs with a spatula. Return the mixing bowl with the eggs and white chocolate to the double boiler for 1 minute to finish cooking the eggs. Stir the chocolate mixture, during the minute of cooking time, and then remove the chocolate mixture from the double boiler.

6. Gently fold the whipped cream into the chocolate mixture with a spatula. Refrigerate the mousse for 3–4 hours, which will thicken once it is cooled.

FOR THE CASHEW BRITTLE

1¼ cup raw cashews

¾ cup brown sugar

½ cup heavy whipping cream

¼ cup unsalted butter

TO MAKE THE CASHEW BRITTLE

1. Preheat the oven to 325°F.

2. Pulse the cashews in a food processor until they are crushed into small pieces, and then set them aside.

3. Place the brown sugar, heavy whipping cream, and butter in a medium-size saucepan over medium heat and stir until the mixture is well incorporated. Continue to stir the mixture frequently, but allow it to thicken.

4. Pour the mixture into a medium sized mixing bowl and combine it with the cashews. Mix everything together.

5. Cut two pieces of parchment paper to fit a baking sheet (about 12 × 18 inches). Place one piece of parchment paper on the baking sheet and coat it with nonstick spray. Pour the caramel-cashew mixture onto the parchment paper and spread it out as much as possible.

6. Coat the remaining piece of parchment paper with nonstick spray and place it sprayed side down on top of the caramel-cashew mixture. Using a rolling pin on top of the top parchment paper, roll out the mixture as thin as possible.

7. Remove the top piece of parchment paper and place the baking sheet in the oven. Bake the mixture for 5 minutes. After 5 minutes of baking, rotate the pan so that the mixture bakes evenly. The cashew brittle is done when it turns a dark caramel color. Remove it from the oven and let it cool in the pan.

3 cups Coconut Tapioca (age 194)

¼ teaspoon lime zest

1. Spoon the Matcha Mousse into a serving bowl.

2. Top the Matcha Mousse with the Coconut Tapioca.

3. Break the Cashew Brittle into large pieces and top the tapioca with the pieces. Sprinkle the lime zest over the tapioca using a microplane.

FRENCH TOAST

Serves 4

My preference has always been a thick French toast that is a little wet in the middle. The trick to making great French toast is to use a thick-cut piece of bread (I like challah) that you've dried out the day before in a warm spot in your kitchen. Drying out the bread will enable it to soak up the custard before you make the dish.

FOR THE COCONUT WHIPPED CREAM

1 cup full-fat coconut milk, chilled (about half a can, 7 ounces)

2 cups heavy whipping cream

½ cup powdered sugar

TO MAKE THE COCONUT WHIPPED CREAM

1. Scoop the solid cream from the can of the chilled coconut milk and place it in a stand mixer.

2. Add the whipping cream to the stand mixer.

3. Turn the stand mixer on and whip the cream for 3–5 minutes until soft peaks form.

4. Add the powdered sugar and mix for an additional 30 seconds.

> If coconut milk does not agree with you, you can use regular whipped cream to make this dessert. Additionally, if you don't have a stand mixer, you can pour all the ingredients into a mixing bowl and use a handheld mixer.

ASSEMBLY

8 large brown eggs

2⅔ cups whole milk

½ cup confectioners' sugar

¾ teaspoon vanilla extract

¾ teaspoon kosher salt

4 (1-inch-thick) slices of challah bread, dried out the day before

1 tablespoon unsalted butter

¼ cup Miso Caramel (page 175)

1 cup Coconut Whipped Cream (recipe above)

¾ cup strawberries, sliced

½ cup blueberries

8–10 leaves of mint, for garnish

1. Place the eggs, milk, ¼ cup of confectioners' sugar, the vanilla extract, and kosher salt in a mixing bowl, and whisk them together. Pour the mixture into a relatively shallow bowl or pie plate that is big enough to fit 4 slices of challah bread.

2. Dip the challah into the custard. If you are using a very shallow bowl, you will be able to submerge the challah bread. Submerge the challah bread for 30 seconds to ensure that the custard soaks into the bread. If you cannot submerge the bread, make sure to dip both sides of the bread into the custard for 30 seconds on each side. Place the dipped challah bread on a roasting rack placed over a rimmed baking sheet. This will allow any excess custard to run off the bread.

3. Heat a large cast iron pan or steel skillet over medium heat and melt the butter. Swirl the pan to make sure the melted butter completely covers the bottom of the pan.

4. Place the slices of challah in the pan. It should take about 8 minutes to cook the French toast from start to finish (about 4 minutes on each side). Of course, the timing may vary depending on how thick the bread is. After about 3 minutes of cooking on one side, use a spatula to look under the bread and check the color. After 4 minutes of cooking, it should be golden brown. Flip the bread with the spatula and cook the other side for 4 minutes.

5. When all the slices of challah are toasted, remove them from the pan and slice them on a diagonal on a cutting board. Shingle the pieces of toast across a large serving plate.

6. Spoon the Miso Caramel and Coconut Whipped Cream into the crevices between the slices of French toast. Garnish the plates with the strawberries and blueberries.

7. Sprinkle the remaining confectioners' sugar on top of the plate and add the mint leaves for additional garnish.

BANANA NUTELLA® SPRING ROLLS

Serves 4

A whimsical, stoner dessert, our Banana Nutella Spring Rolls have been a constant on our restaurant menu since our opening night. They are also a hit as late-night snacks for all the weddings we cater from the trucks.

FOR THE SPRING ROLL

1 medium-size banana

12 spring roll wrappers

1 egg, beaten

½ cup Nutella

TO MAKE THE SPRING ROLL

1. Slice the banana in half. Then, slice each half once again to make 4 quarters. Slice each quarter into 3 "spears." (You should have 12 "spears" altogether—one for each spring roll wrapper.)

2. Place a spring roll wrapper flat on a cutting board or on the counter, with one pointed end facing toward you. Brush the beaten egg on all the edges of the wrapper.

3. Place a banana spear in the center of the wrapper.

4. Schmear 2 teaspoons of Nutella onto the wrapper right next to the banana.

5. Roll up the spring roll wrapper like a burrito. Start by placing the wrapper in a diamond shape, with one of the four points directly pointed at your chest. Fold the left and right points in toward the center of the spring roll. Parts of the wrapper will cover the banana Nutella mixture and you will only have two points sticking out (the top and bottom). Fold the bottom point that is closest to your chest toward the center of the spring roll and tuck it underneath the other sides and the filling. Roll the sides away from you until the spring roll is closed and folds up like a burrito.

ASSEMBLY

2 quarts vegetable oil

Confectioners' sugar, for garnish

¼ teaspoon lime zest

1 cup Coconut Whipped Cream (page 198)

1. Pour the oil into a Dutch oven, a large cast iron skillet, or a deep fryer and place it over high heat. Bring the temperature of the oil to 350°F. Use a candy thermometer to check the temperature of the oil.

2. Once the oil is at temperature, carefully place the spring rolls into the oil. It should take about $1^{1}/_{2}$–2 minutes to fry each of the spring rolls (they'll turn golden brown when they're done).

3. After they are done, remove the spring rolls from the oil and place them on a plate covered with paper towels.

4. Stack the spring rolls on a platter, top them with confectioners' sugar and lime zest, and serve them with a side of Coconut Whipped Cream.

10

COCKTAILS

Opposite: A busy Friday night at the bar, where the action is nonstop.

One of my biggest fears in opening the restaurant was creating a cocktail program from scratch. I had very limited bar or cocktail knowledge, and here we were gunning to open a full bar with a sophisticated array of cocktails. I interviewed a bunch of candidates for the bar manager position and the final choice came down to two candidates one of whom was Kevin Kok, our current beverage director. I did not, however, offer the job to Kevin. I offered it to the other candidate, and, luckily, Kevin agreed to come on board as a bartender. Kevin ended up taking over the bar manager position before we even opened our doors, and we've never looked back. I completely misfired by not hiring Kevin for the position right off the bat. I'll admit when I've been wrong, and I was wrong.

I always tease Kevin about his second interview with me, where I asked him to make a couple drinks that he could see fitting into the restaurant. Kevin came to the interview with a recipe book that was about a hundred pages long. He rummaged through it and told me about all the cocktails he knew how to make, including ones he'd created at his old bar in Oregon. For the interview, Kevin came prepared to make an Asian pear vodka cocktail, among others. I must have come off as intimidating, because the man couldn't pour a cocktail to save his life. Half of it poured out of the cocktail shaker onto the table. His face turned bright red and he apologized.

To this day, I don't know why Kevin had such a bad case of the shakes—but he's never had them again! We still have a good laugh about it to this day. All joking aside, as we've grown the business, Kevin has become a huge asset. He truly loves cocktails, and when he's home alone at night, I imagine him leafing through his hundred-page recipe book, like Bill Belichick looking through football plays, to figure out which drink will be the one to win over his next customer.

THE VIOLET'S DREAM

If you want to impress someone with your cocktail-making skills, this is definitely the one to show off. The roasted-beet shrub gives the drink a beautiful, deep-purple color, while the egg white provides a layer of whipped foam to top it off. Gin pairs incredibly well with the beet shrub, making this cocktail go down smoothly.

FOR THE ROASTED-BEET SHRUB

Makes about 3 cups

1 pound small red beets, washed

2 cups sugar

1¾ cup apple cider vinegar

¼ cup balsamic vinegar

TO MAKE THE ROASTED-BEET SHRUB

1. Preheat the oven to 350°F.

2. Wrap the beets individually in foil and roast them in the oven for 45 minutes.

3. Remove the beets from the oven and let them cool down until they are cool enough to peel. Peel the beets and discard the skins. Pulse the beets in a food processor for 10–15 seconds. You may need to stop and open the lid to the food processor to push the beets down that are stuck to the side of the machine. Remove the beets and place them in a small plastic container. Add the sugar to the beets until the sugar is fully incorporated. The sugar should dissolve in the beets and the beet juice since they will still both be relatively warm.

4. Place the beets in the refrigerator for 3 days to allow them to ferment. After each day, make sure to remove the beet mixture from the refrigerator and mix it by hand to ensure that all residual sugar has dissolved.

5. After the beet mixture has fermented for 3 days, strain the liquid from the mixture using a fine mesh strainer and discard the solids.

6. Add the apple cider vinegar and balsamic vinegar to the strained beet liquid. Refrigerate the beet shrub in an airtight container for up to 1 month.

FOR THE LAVENDER SYRUP

2 tablespoons dry lavender petals

½ cup sugar

¾ cup water

TO MAKE THE LAVENDER SYRUP

1. Place all the ingredients in a small saucepan and bring the mixture to a boil over medium-high heat.

2. Once the mixture boils, reduce the heat and let the syrup simmer for 20 minutes.

3. Strain the lavender petals from the syrup and place the syrup in an airtight container in the refrigerator.

ASSEMBLY

2 ounces gin

¾ ounce roasted-beet shrub

¾ ounce egg white

½ ounce Lavender Syrup (recipe above)

½ ounce lemon juice

1. Place all the ingredients in a shaker and filled with a scoop of ice. Shake vigorously for 10 seconds.

2. Strain the liquid into a separate mixing glass and discard the ice.

3. Pour the strained liquid back into the shaker and dry-shake it (that is, shake it without ice) for another 20 seconds to aerate the foam in the egg whites and create a thicker foam. Double-strain (see Note) the liquid into an champagne coupe.

Note *To double-strain, use the strainer on the cocktail shaker as well as a fine-mesh strainer over the glass.*

THE COSMONAUT

Makes 1 drink

This refreshing drink riffs on the traditional Cosmopolitan cocktail with a splash of bubbly. The Cosmonaut is the perfect cocktail for birthday parties and wedding or baby showers—partly because it's served in a champagne flute, which doesn't tip over as easily as the stemmed, V-shaped cocktail glass in which the Cosmopolitan is traditionally served—and partly because the drink is so easy to prep and execute.

FOR THE POMEGRANATE SYRUP

½ cup 100% pomegranate juice

½ cup sugar

2 teaspoons pomegranate molasses

1½ teaspoons orange blossom water

TO MAKE THE POMEGRANATE SYRUP

Place all the ingredients in a medium-size saucepan and bring the mixture to a boil. After the mixture has boiled, turn off the heat and let the syrup cool to room temperature. Place the syrup in an airtight container and refrigerate.

ASSEMBLY

1 ounce vodka

¾ ounce ginger liqueur

¾ ounce lime juice

½ ounce Pomegranate Syrup

Prosecco, for topping the drink

1. Pour the vodka, ginger liqueur, lime juice, and Pomegranate Syrup into a shaker filled with a scoop of ice and shake the mixture vigorously for 10 seconds.

2. Strain the liquid into a champagne flute and top off the drink with the Prosecco.

TOKYO SOUR

Makes 1 drink

The Japanese have been producing commercial whiskey for over ninety years. In the past five to ten years, the top Japanese whiskies have become renowned everywhere. For the purposes of this cocktail, a Japanese blended whiskey, as opposed to a Scotch whiskey, will work perfectly. The Japanese have really mastered the art and craft of whiskey blending, the main driver behind the current popularity of Japanese whiskey.

FOR THE SIMPLE SYRUP

½ cup sugar

TO MAKE THE SIMPLE SYRUP

1. Place the sugar and ¾ cup of water in a medium-size saucepan and bring the mixture to a boil over medium-high heat.

2. Once the simple syrup boils, turn off the heat and allow the syrup to cool to room temperature. Place the syrup in an airtight container and refrigerate.

ASSEMBLY

2 ounces Japanese blended whiskey

¾ ounce lemon juice

¾ ounce Simple Syrup

¾ ounce egg white (approximately 1 medium-size egg white)

1 dash Angostura® aromatic bitters

1. Place all the ingredients into a shaker with a scoop of ice, and shake vigorously for 10 seconds.

2. Strain the liquid into a separate mixing glass. Discard the ice from the shaker.

3. Pour the liquid back into the shaker and dry-shake the liquid (shaking the liquid without ice) for another 20 seconds to aerate the foam in the egg whites and create a thicker foam.

4. Double-strain (see Note, page 208) the liquid into a champagne coupe.

> For added effect, add another dash of Angostura bitters on top of the foam which sits on top of the drink. Using a toothpick, draw a design in the foam on top of the cocktail, if you like.

WASABI MARY

The Wasabi Mary is a really fun play on the standard Bloody Mary. Wasabi adds an extra horseradish kick. I always joke that the Wasabi Mary concocted by our beverage director, Kevin Kok, is a meal on top of a meal. The drink itself is savory and combines a lot of flavors, but it's also topped with all kinds of pickled goodies that pair beautifully with the drink itself.

FOR THE THAI CHILI– AND THAI BASIL–INFUSED VODKA

Makes 1 cup

1 cup vodka

2 Thai Chilies, whole (see Asian Food Glossary, page 219)

½ cup Thai basil leaves

TO MAKE THE THAI CHILI– AND THAI BASIL–INFUSED VODKA

1. Place the Thai chilis, Thai basil, and vodka in a small, lidded mason jar or airtight container. Infuse them for 1 week.

2. After 1 week, strain the Thai chilies and Thai basil from the vodka.

FOR THE WASABI MARY MIX

Makes 4 servings

½ teaspoon granulated garlic

½ teaspoon freshly ground black pepper

½ teaspoon celery salt

½ teaspoon kosher salt

½ teaspoon prepared horseradish

½ cup lemon juice

½ cup olive juice

¼ cup red wine

¼ cup Worcestershire sauce

2¼ cups tomato juice

½ habanero chili pepper, seeds removed and diced

1 tablespoon habanero hot sauce

1 tablespoon prepared wasabi

TO MAKE THE WASABI MARY MIX

Stir all the ingredients together in a pitcher.

ASSEMBLY

¼ English (seedless) cucumber, sliced into ½-inch rounds

½ lime, cut into ½-inch slices

½ lemon, cut into ½-inch slices

¼ cup kosher salt

2 ounces Thai Chili– (see Asian Food Glossary, page 219) and Thai Basil–Infused Vodka

1 cup Wasabi Mary Mix

¼ cup Japanese Sesame Pickles (page 171) (optional)

1. Make a small cut in each piece of English cucumber. The cut should be half the diameter of the cucumber slice.

2. Make another small cut in the middle of the flesh of each lime and lemon slice, making sure not to pierce the skin. This will allow the lime and lemon slices to sit on the rim of each pint glass.

3. Salt a pint glass with the kosher salt and add ice to the glass.

4. Pour the vodka and Wasabi Mary Mix over the ice.

5. Garnish the pint glass by wedging the cucumber, lemon, and lime slices on the rim of the glass. Top the Bloody Mary with the pickles.

. . . .

Note Other pickled vegetables can be used as garnish.

. . . .

ESPRESSO ALEXANDER

Makes 2 cups

One of the better coffee cocktails around, the Espresso Alexander delivers a double fix of caffeine and booze. Served cold, it is the perfect cocktail for the summer months.

FOR THE ESPRESSO VODKA

2 cups vodka

2 ounces espresso beans, whole

TO MAKE THE ESPRESSO VODKA

1. Soak the espresso beans in the vodka in a small, lidded mason jar or airtight container. Refrigerate the mixture for 16–20 hours.

2. Strain the mixture into a pitcher and reserve some of the espresso beans for the garnish.

ASSEMBLY

1 ounce Espresso Vodka

1 ounce coffee liqueur

1 ounce half-and-half

1. Place all the ingredients in a shaker with ice and shake vigorously for 10 seconds.

2. Double-strain the liquid (see Note, page 208) into a martini glass and garnish the drink with 3 coffee beans.

SANGRIA

Serves 8

Sangria is an easy drink to batch for dinner parties. What makes this sangria unique, however, is the blend of wines, rum, strawberry shrub, and a splash of champagne. If you have a vintage punch bowl, use it for the sangria so your guests can serve themselves.

FOR THE STRAWBERRY SHRUB

Makes about 1 cup

½ pound strawberries, washed and ends removed, sliced ¼ inch thick

½ cup sugar

⅓ cup white wine vinegar

TO MAKE THE STRAWBERRY SHRUB

1. Mix the sliced strawberries with the sugar in a large airtight plastic container and allow the mixture to ferment in the refrigerator for 3 days.

2. After each day, make sure to stir the mixture by hand to ensure that all the residual sugar has dissolved.

3. After the strawberry mixture has fermented, strain the liquid using a fine mesh strainer. The liquid can be strained into any airtight vessel you have on hand.

4. Add the white wine vinegar to the strained liquid. Store the shrub for up to 2 weeks in your refrigerator.

ASSEMBLY

10 strawberries, washed, ends removed, and diced

1 Granny Smith apple, peeled and diced

4 ounces light rum

12 ounces Pinot Grigio

12 ounces rosé

8 ounces orange juice

4 ounces Lavender Syrup (page 207)

4 ounces Strawberry Shrub

12 ounces ginger beer (preferably Fever-Tree®)

12 ounces champagne

Fresh fruit of choice for garnish

1. Place all the ingredients, except the champagne, into a large glass pitcher. Cover the pitcher. Let the ingredients sit overnight, then strain the fruits from the liquid. Discard the fruit.

2. Add the champagne to give the sangria some fizz.

3. Serve the sangria over ice in a wine glass and garnish the glasses with your choice of fresh fruit.

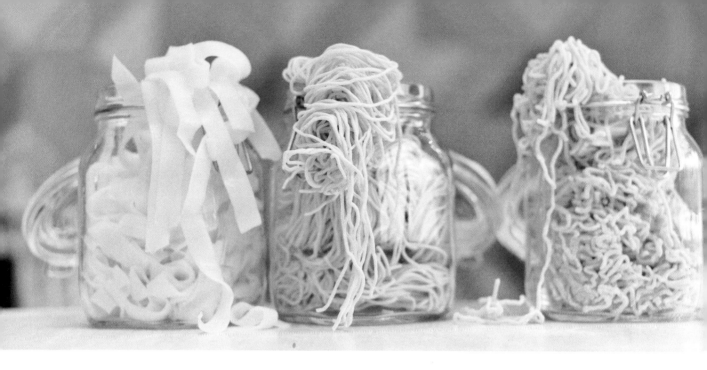

NOODLE GLOSSARY

There are so many Asian noodles out there that you can get lost looking for the appropriate noodle for a recipe. To make the search a little easier, I've listed a few types of noodles below that are called for in the recipes in this book. Your grocery store may not carry them, however, so your best bet is to go to an Asian specialty grocery store, like 99 Ranch Market, H Mart, or a similar, local store. For online sources, see www.seriouseats.com, which carries an entire glossary of Asian noodles.

Banh Pho Noodles (sometimes referred to as Pad Thai or rice stick noodles) These flat rice noodles are used for Pad Thai. They need to be parsoaked in hot water and then strained before you cook them in a wok or pan. You can parsoak Banh Pho Noodles ahead of time, since they don't stick together very much when they are cold.

Above: From left to right ho fun noodle, tonkotsu ramen noodles, Tokyo wavy ramen noodles.

216

Chajang Noodles Used traditionally with chajangmyun (a black bean and pork based sauce), these noodles are thick and made out of wheat flour. These make for a good alternative for Dan Dan Noodles if you cannot find the wheat Quon Yick noodles since they provide a nice amount of surface area for the sauce to cover them.

Ho Fun Noodles These flat, wide rice noodles are used in Chinese and Vietnamese food. They are sold fresh in blocks. You will need to hand-peel these noodles to separate them into individual strands. The best way to do that is to remove the noodles from the package and microwave them for 1 minute. This will soften them up and make them easier to peel off the block. You can find these noodles at your local Chinese grocery store (99 Ranch Market, H Mart, etc.).

Pancit Canton Noodles These are egg-based noodles that are perfect for stir-fried noodle dishes, and are easily sourced at most Asian grocery stores. Pancit Canton Noodles are a great choice for Laksa as well (page 17). Pancit Canton Noodles have a soft texture and soak up sauces quickly. Keep your eye on these noodles to make sure you don't overcook them.

Ramen Noodles Even though Ramen Noodles have become mainstream in so many parts of the United States, finding good Ramen Noodles is still difficult. Sun Noodles, the biggest ramen manufacturer in the United States, primarily sells its product to distributors who in turn sell to restaurants. You should be able to find Sun's frozen ramen product in the noodle section at larger Asian grocery stores, however. Each of these frozen ramen packs spells out what recipe they are meant for (i.e., Shoyu, Tonkotsu, TanTan Men, etc.). Thaw the ramen packs overnight in your refrigerator and they should be good to go the next day. Ramen Noodles come in all kinds of shapes and sizes. Thicker Ramen Noodles are meant for tsukumen (dipping ramen) and are great for mazamen (brothless ramen). Some of the thinner noodles, like tonkotsu, are meant for heavier, pork-based broths.

Wheat Noodles We use Quon Yick wheat noodles (a San Francisco-based brand). These noodles are great for dan dan, ginger scallion, and other types of Chinese-inspired noodle dishes. I like these noodles because they don't stick together, whether they are hot or cold.

ASIAN FOOD GLOSSARY

I t's no secret that Asian grocery stores can be intimidating. When you first walk in, you're hit with the smell of raw fish, pork, and stinky tofu. Immediately, your senses are thrown off. Before you even get to the packaged products, you realize you can't buy fish by the filet, the poultry section doesn't carry organic chicken thighs, and there aren't many people in the store who speak English. This glossary will help you navigate Asian grocery stores and become familiar with many of their products. With each visit, it'll become easier to find what you're looking for—enjoy the adventure.

Amasu Shoga You are probably already familiar with this sweet pickled ginger product from eating sushi at Japanese restaurants. This product is relatively mainstream and can be found at most American grocery stores.

Aonori This dried, flaky Japanese seaweed is great on top of okonomiyaki and yakisoba. You can typically find it in a small bottle that weighs less than 1 ounce.

Black Bean Dace See *Fried Dace*.

Black Vinegar This vinegar carries a smokier flavor than rice wine vinegar. Black vinegar is popular in Northern China and is typically made from sorghum. Pair it with soy sauce and use it as a dipping sauce for dumplings.

Bonito Flakes If you want to get super-concentrated Bonito Flakes, you can always purchase your own whole dried bonito and shave it in a bonito box (see page 30). Otherwise, you can purchase shaved dried fish flakes in bags as small as 2–3 ounces. The Japanese top off a lot of dishes with Bonito Flakes, including okonomiyaki and takoyaki, and use it as a core ingredient in making dashi.

Chili Garlic Sauce Chili garlic sauce has made its way into the mainstream and can be found at almost any grocery store these days. The commercial product is not nearly as good as homemade sambal or fermented chili, but in a pinch it's a worthy product paired with noodle and rice dishes and stir-fries.

Chinese Five-Spice Powder A powder that is comprised of star anise, cloves, Chinese cinnamon, Sichuan pepper, and fennel seeds.

Dark Soy Sauce (also called mushroom soy) There are a variety of brands on the market. I prefer Pearl River Bridge® because it is a very dark soy sauce (darker than most). Proteins will take on the color of the dark soy when you use it for braises.

Fish Cakes Typically found in the frozen food section, these fish cakes are comprised mainly of whitefish and are fried before they are packaged. They pair great as an add-on for soup noodle dishes.

Fish Sauce Made from fermented anchovies and salt, there are a number of fish sauces currently on the market. For a midlevel brand I would recommend Mega-Chef®. Of course, you could always purchase a bottle of Red Boat® (top level) or Squid® (lower midlevel).

Fried Dace A long time ago, the Chinese decided to fry these little fish and store them in black bean sauce. You can find black bean dace in yellow-colored containers at most Asian grocery stores.

Fried Shallots These shallots fried in palm oil come prepackaged and will stay good for months in their original sealed plastic container. They are great sprinkled on top of dishes to add an extra layer of crunch. Honestly, I see no need to fry your own shallots when you can buy these.

Furikake This dried condiment from Japan comes in a variety of flavors and incorporates bonito, sesame seeds, sugar, and salt. Egg furikake (dehydrated egg furikake) and salmon furikake are my favorites.

Gochujang This Korean red chili paste is great in marinades or used on its own as a condiment. Since the flavor can be overpowering, I think it's best to mix it with another condiment, like doenjang (fermented bean paste) or red miso.

Hoisin Sauce A thick soybean based sauce that is dark and sweet. Used in stir fries and in sauces for vegetables, it also pairs nicely with crispy duck (moo shu style) and pork belly (think bao buns).

Japanese Sesame Paste. Also known as "Neri Goma," you can find Japanese sesame paste at specialty Japanese grocery stores. If you don't have time to head to a Japanese grocer or can't find one, just use tahini as a substitute. Or, you can always make your own with toasted white sesame seeds and a touch of non-flavored oil in a small food processor.

Katsuobushi. See *Bonito Flakes*.

Kewpie Mayonnaise® There's a rumor floating around that Kewpie Mayo no longer contains MSG. Whether it does or doesn't, it doesn't really matter. This is the most distinctive mayo on the market, and the Japanese put it on everything. I recommend buying OG Kewpie Mayonnaise that comes with a red top inside a plastic bag. Use it on a sandwich or a hot dog, or squirt some on your onigiri.

Kochukaru Flakes Korean red pepper flakes can be found in small or large bags at your local Korean grocery store. They're essential for all kimchis.

Kombu This dried seaweed forms the base of our recipe for Dashi (page 167), which then forms the base for all our ramen recipes. Kombu is high in natural glutamic acid, a key component of monosodium glutamate (MSG). In other words, kombu is MSG without the high salt content.

Lap Cheong This dried Chinese sausage can be found at most Chinese and Asian grocery stores. It comes prepackaged, with 8–10 links in each package. The pork-based sausage is sweetened and smoked.

Mae Ploy Mae Ploy is one of those sweet chili sauce staples that has made its way into most grocery stores. It's great as a dipping sauce for spring rolls (fried or chilled). We use it only in our "Peached Sauce" for the Social Burger (page 63). I recommend using Thai Chili Dipping Sauce (page 182) for the Mom's Shrimp Toast recipe (page 40) instead of Mae Ploy.

Mirin A sweet rice wine that the Japanese use in a lot of marinades and sauces. We use it as an ingredient in our Korean Steak Marinade (page 101) and also our Tare (page 157).

Miso If you're shopping at a large grocery or health food store, you'll likely find white (shiro) miso and possibly red miso, and of course you can find it in any Asian food market. Miso is made from fermented soybeans and will last in the fridge for up to 4 months.

Nori Also known as dried seaweed, nori can take on a lot of different shapes and sizes and be used in a variety of manners. You can typically find nori in large dried sheets at most grocery stores, and you can also find it in strips at speciality Asian grocers.

Okonomiyaki Sauce Similar to tonkatsu sauce, okonomiyaki sauce is sweet and incorporates ketchup, Worcestershire sauce, honey, and soy sauce. It's best to go to a Japanese specialty grocery store to find this sauce.

Oyster Sauce Oyster Sauce uses oyster extract to give a punch of umami flavor to stir-fried noodle and fried rice dishes. You could make your own Oyster Sauce, but honestly it'd be like making ketchup. What's the point? Most of these products contain MSG and I'm okay with that.

Pickled Mustard Greens These salty pickled greens add some funk to Sichuan dishes and an extra layer of flavor to many others.

Rice Paper Wrappers The rice paper wrappers that are called for in the recipes in this book are the kind that are used to make cold Vietnamese spring rolls.

Rice Wine Vinegar A delicate vinegar made by fermenting the sugars from rice, rice wine vinegar serves as a great pickling liquid and can also be used in Asian-inspired vinaigrettes.

Sake Also known as Japanese rice wine, sake is incredibly versatile as an ingredient in marinades and also for Tare. You can use either drinking sake or cooking tare for the recipes in this book.

Salted Shrimp The Chinese and Koreans use dried and salted shrimp in a ton of recipes, including kimchi and dipping pastes. Salted shrimp pack a very strong, briny shrimp flavor.

Sambal Oelek Sambal is one of the more popular ground chili pastes that can be found at the majority of grocery stores. It is a little hotter than chili garlic paste, which can be found directly next to Sambal on store shelves.

Shaoxing Wine A must for Chinese stir-fries, this amber-colored wine is made from fermented rice and is super-fragrant.

Shiro Miso See *Miso*.

Shredded Nori We use this dried seaweed product as a topping on some of our dishes, including the Yume Dog (page 61). Nori appears in several different forms in this glossary so, the moral of the story is, buy some nori and keep it handy in your kitchen.

Shrimp Paste This condiment is used in a lot of Filipino and Malaysian cooking. It has a strong presence in Laksa (page 17). You can purchase shrimp paste in a small 4-ounce container, which should be enough for any recipe that calls for it. At the restaurant, we like Por Kwan brand—the one with the shrimp on the label. I prefer to purchase shrimp paste that has a mixture of oil and a wet paste, rather than the dry blocks of paste (think Asian shrimp bouillon blocks) you can sometimes find at Asian grocery stores.

Sichuan Peppercorns Most high-end grocery stores carry this product in their section designated for bulk spices. At the restaurant, we always toast peppercorns before using them in a recipe. Toasted and ground, they are great sprinkled on top of a spicy Sichuan-inspired dish or used whole in Sichuan Chili Oil (page 180).

Spring Roll Wrappers In the recipes for spring rolls in this book, you are given the option to purchase either spring roll wrappers (for the rice puffs), used for cold spring rolls, or wrappers that are used for deep-fried spring rolls. I recommend Spring Home brand® for deep-fried spring rolls. These wrappers are referred to as "spring roll pastry wrappers" and contain eggs. You can stuff them with either sweet or savory fillings.

Sriracha Sauce At this point, sriracha is pretty much a standard chili sauce that can be found in almost everyone's home kitchen. It's still a great go-to when you need some spice in a pinch.

Star Anise Anise, which is one of the ingredients in Chinese five-spice powder, is effective all on its own, as a whole ingredient that adds great flavor to braises. Whenever possible, I toast it to bring out even more flavor. Most American grocery stores carry star anise pods.

Sweet Soy Sauce Healthy Boy brand makes a great sweet soy sauce. It's one of those magical, super-thick, molasses-y sauces that tastes like licorice on the back end.

Tamarind Concentrate Instead of getting your hands super-sticky picking through a block of pure tamarind pulp, tamarind concentrate gives you the flavor of tamarind in a liquid format ready to incorporate into your recipes. A lot of regular grocery stores are starting to carry this product, but you can find it at most Asian grocery stores as well. Tamarind offers a sour and sweet flavor that helps to bolster a lot of traditional Thai recipes.

Tempura Flour You could always make tempura batter from scratch using a mixture of rice flour and all-purpose flour, but the packaged tempura flour does the job really well. Whisk it with very cold sparkling water and you're set. Tempura flour can be found in most American grocery stores.

Thai Chilies These dried chilies pack a punch and really amp up dishes like our Pad Thai Sauce (page 106). A little goes a long way, so you'll likely need just an ounce or so, depending on how many people there are on your guest list.

Tobanjan Also known as doubanjiang, this chili bean paste is used in a lot of Chinese and Japanese recipes. I prefer the Youki brand, which has a distinctive fermented bean taste and a strong, but not overpowering, chili flavor.

Togarashi. A classic Japanese condiment seen on the table at most ramen houses, Togarashi is an amalgam of powdered chili pepper, orange peel, sesame seeds, Japanese pepper, ginger, and seaweed.

Wasabi Powder. Also known as Japanese horseradish, wasabi can be found at most Asian grocery stores. Typically, you will have the option to purchase wasabi paste or powder. The powdered version will keep longer, and you can just mix it with water when you need it to form a paste.

Yuzu Juice Yuzu is a Japanese citrus fruit that has a very distinctive and strong flavor profile. A little goes a long way. You can typically find Yuzu Juice at most Asian grocery stores or Japanese specialty stores. Some high-end yuzu products can cost as much as $50 a bottle.

ACKNOWLEDGMENTS

I would have never been in the position to write this book were it not for the support of my wife, Kris, my family, and the few friends of mine who believed in me enough to invest in my food truck back in 2010. I can honestly say that I would not have a business today without their continued support. There have been many dark days trying to get this business profitable and moving in the right direction. Days where I did not want to continue and wanted to throw in the towel. They kept pushing and supporting me, and I am forever grateful for their support.

I also want to thank my staff and loyal employees. You know who you are and what it took to grow this thing from a tiny operation into what it is today. An owner can only do so much for a business before he turns the keys over to his staff to run it. There is beauty in the process and journey and I thank you for appreciating that beauty.

Thank you to my agent, Jennifer Chen Tran, who never let this book dream die. We journeyed over four years together and multiple iterations to see this book come to light. Thanks for pushing me when I did not really want to push further.

Thank you to Era Ceramics for allowing me to feature its amazing plateware throughout this book, and Hana Supermarket, for opening up its doors and providing a backdrop for some awesome product shots.

ABOUT THE AUTHOR

Eric Silverstein was born in Tokyo, Japan and spent eleven years growing up and traveling throughout Asia. He was born into a multi-cultural family, raised by his Chinese mother and Jewish American father. Eric moved stateside in 1995, spending his next six years in Atlanta, Georgia. Eric then pursued a legal career and attended Washington University in St. Louis law school, after which he practiced as a litigator in St. Louis, Missouri.

In 2010, Eric quit his job as a lawyer and founded The Peached Tortilla food truck in Austin, Texas. The Peached Tortilla quickly grew from one food truck to two trucks, then into a full service catering company, multiple brick and mortar locations and an event space. Throughout this continued growth, Eric's focus has been on cooking modern Asian comfort food largely influenced by his upbringing.

When Eric is not working, he enjoys spending time with his family and dog. He is also an avid Atlanta sports fan and continues to wait for the city's first sports championship since 1995.

1st row, left to right: Alicia Gonzales, Alisha Baker, Arti Bhakta, Gilberto "Beto" Solis
2nd row, left to right: Blake Bilodeau, Carolyn Curran, Cecilia Limon, Cheryl Nichols
3rd row, left to right: Edgar Rico, Enrique "Kike" Cruz, James Sanders, Jenna Paul
4th row, left to right: Yat "Kevin" Kok, Kondja Kamatuka, Lora Null, Louise Jewell

1st row, left to right: Marianna Jimenez, Richard Uranga, Roslyn Barrutia
2nd row, left to right: Roman Aguirre, Sarafina Riskind, Stephani O'Connor
3rd row, left to right (in truck): Jesse Herrera, Ryan Rosen, Eamon Burrows, Matt Lee

INDEX